ALTOGETHER
FORGIVEN

Altogether Forgiven

By
Martha Kilpatrick

Shulamite Ministries
SUCHES, GEORGIA

ISBN-13 978-1-936057-37-5
ISBN-10 1-936057-37-9

Altogether Forgiven

Shulamite Ministries
PO Box 10
Suches, GA 30572
www.shulamite.com

Printed in the United States of America.

More Titles by Martha Kilpatrick

Books

Adoration
All and Only
Chariot of Fire
The Mystery of Discipleship

Booklet Series

Knowing God
The Great Lie
Eternal Power
Foundation of Repentance
Powers of the Universe
The Separator
Loved of God

Loving God
Seeing Him
Do You Love Me?
Marys Who Loved Him
Why Am I?
Who Do You Love?
God's Sovereignty

Hearing God
Required as Vital
Power of Decision
The Secret to Answered Prayer
The Hidden Life
The Inner Room
Consider the Lily

Individual Booklets

Surprised by God
The Secret to Fullness
Kingdom Safety
Kingdom Children

Visit Shulamite.com to access the many free online resources from Martha and Shulamite Ministries, including podcasts, a blog, daily devotions and the Martha Kilpatrick Online Library at ReadMK.com!

Statement of Faith

Jesus Christ, the only begotten Son of God,
came in the flesh, shed His holy Blood on the
Cross at Calvary for the sins of the world.
He is Lord of the Universe, King of Kings...

and I am His Shulamite.

Martha Kilpatrick

*I will praise You, O Lord, with my whole heart;
I will show forth
(recount and tell aloud)
all Your marvelous works and wonderful deeds!*
Psalm 9:1 AMPC

TABLE OF CONTENTS

Statement of Faith vii
Foreword xiii

The Miracle of Forgiveness

Miraculous Forgiveness 17
The Most Wonderful News 19
The Legal Universe 23
So Great a Salvation 31

The Cross of Jesus

Jesus Paid It All 37
Today Paradise 43
Who Murdered Jesus? 53
Priceless Blood 57
The End of Satan 63
The Glory of the Cross 69

What Has God Forgiven?

What is Sin? 73
The Murder of God 77
Perfect Forgiveness 87
God's Longing to Forgive 99
Humility is the Lamb 101

Repentance

To Repent Is a Command 105
No Repentance, No Love 111
A Broken Heart for Sin 123
Repentance Lost, Mercy Found 127
Chastened by Love 133

Foundation of Forgiveness

Forgiveness Is 139
The First Forgiveness 141
Why and How 147
Faith and Mountains 155

Your Worst Enemy 161
Offended With God 165
Have You Forgiven God? 169
A Matter of the Heart 173

The Biblical Map of Forgiveness

The Little Child Forgives 179
Like Father, Like Son 191
How Many Times? 195
Confronting the Sinner 197
Lovers of Self 209
The Torturers 215
Glorious Reconciliation 221

A Power We Don't Know

Casting Out the Accuser 227
How to Love Your Enemy 229
True Power, Divine Test 233
Reigning Grace 237

Refusing to Forgive

Hamlet, Revenge and Power 247
Pride Is 255
Bitterness Is 257

The Unoffended

Expectations Lead to Offenses 261
Trust in God Alone 267
Disentangled Soldier 271
The Strange Humility of Jesus 279

Living Forgiving

A Living Sacrifice 287
Prison Breakout 291
Humility Is… 305
Living in Grace 307
Forgiveness and Healing 309

The Mystery of the Cross

Seeking the Cross 317

Uunfixable Humanity 323

The Perfect Man 327

What Did the Cross Finish? 329

It Is Finished

Divine Abiding 337

The Startling Little Word 339

Another Life Lives 341

Jesus' Great Assignments 345

God on the Throne

His Perfection in Suffering 351

Sovereign Offenses 357

Created Days 361

No Other God 365

The Potter and the Wheel 367

Living Epistles

Joseph and Destiny 375

Daniel and Worship 387

The End of David's Story 393

You Are a Love Story 397

Afterword 403

Author's Notes 409

Foreword

To know Jesus will cost
you *everything*.

You will have to
forgive everything.

You will have to
accept everything.

You will have to
give up everything!

But you will have the pearl,
THE PEARL,
whose price is
unsearchable and inestimable.

**You will know the only
glory that a person can experience,
to love and be loved by our Heavenly Father.**

*When he found one priceless pearl,
he went and sold everything he had
and bought it.
Matthew 13:46 HCSB*

Christ is the Pearl, worth any price.

Martha Kilpatrick

The Miracle of Forgiveness

A relentless Love, so vast and immeasurable,
gave everything for you.

Jesus died your death-in-sin, to the ultimate grave.
The Father sent His suffering to the hideous end.
The Holy Spirit raised Him to Unconquerable Life
and you were miraculously solved. For Always.

Miraculous Forgiveness

We are all on a lifelong journey and the core of its challenge, the terrible demand of its centrality is forgiving and being forgiven.

By that rocky and formidable climb – the sweat of forgiveness – we can peak the mountain of human suffering and gaze down on the meaning of our own history.

For every believer, wrongs are a life-long challenge. There is no harder work in life than to forgive. It is a Labor so hard that few will work the work, which is to say, "Die the death."

Only by our own forgiveness will we comprehend the Ghastly Cross and our Bloody Savior's gift of innocence.

Innocence quite beyond forgiveness.
Given to me, to all.

I am a shameful expert in bitterness. I am all too familiar with its dark paths and soul-traps. I know the ruts it carves in your mind that your thoughts find so easily, so habitually.

I am also acquainted with the alienation from God that is the reward of unforgiveness.

Bitterness has been my torment and, in the end, my crucible of spiritual freedom. It brought me to beg the Lord to make me more an expert on forgiveness than bitterness.

I know that my own story,
    when it's finished, is going to be
        only about God's grace and forgiveness,
           not my achievement or any honors.

One measure of a life's spiritual success will
    – in the end of all –
    be the size of genuine forgiveness.

So I asked the Lord for rich secrets of forgiveness. And I
discovered the one secret that is the key to all—
    to forgiving and being forgiven.

That secret is love.

I tell you the secret at the beginning and then I will let
the Secret unfold Himself . . .

Come with me, beloved of God,
    come with me to behold with new eyes,
        the miracle of the universe – forgiveness.

And here it is, the Miracle of Forgiveness . . .

You were dead because of your sins
and because your sinful nature was not yet cut away.
Then God made you alive with Christ,
for he forgave all our sins.
He canceled the record of the charges against us
and took it away by nailing it to the cross.
Colossians 2:13-14 NLT

The Most Wonderful News

The gospel means "good news." What exactly IS the good news?

John the Baptist looked up from the river of his labors into the face of Jesus, his cousin, coming down to the water. Jesus was there to fulfill God's commands without exception, humbly asking to be baptized of John.

John, son of Elizabeth, knew Jesus' story and had probably witnessed His strange goodness, but still did not know fully His Identity.

> *I have need to be baptized by You,*
> *and do You come to me?*
> *Matthew 3:14 NASB*

John nonetheless obeyed the Holy Man and plunged Him under the running water.

Out of the river, Jesus rose to what was – even to the Son of God – a new and power-filled life!

The Gentle Presence of the Holy Spirit descended on Him, "in bodily form like a dove" (Luke 3:22 NIV), and abided with Him. By this Divine Imbuing, of which he had been told (John 1:3-34), John knew for certain then that Jesus was the Promised Messiah.

And with a simple introduction of just one sentence, John then declared one of the most awesome statements ever uttered by a mere human.

Behold! The Lamb of God
who takes away the sin of the world!
John 1:29 NKJV

What an amazing thing that John the Baptist understood this fully. He knew the breadth and scope of forgiveness even before it took place on the Cross! We don't comprehend it even though we *know* it has happened.

This gospel news is mankind's greatest need
by the threat of darkest hell.

The Lamb of God *"takes away the sin of the world."*

What a thought! Not forgiven only . . .
That would be phenomenal in itself.
But to "take away" all our sin.
Can we comprehend it?

"Take away" is the Greek word *airo*: to lift, to take up or away, away with, bear up, carry, lift up, loose, put away, remove (Strong's #142).

For I will be merciful toward their iniquities,
and I will remember their sins no more.
Hebrews 8:12 ESV

Oh such news! My sin is not just paid for,
and I am not only ransomed and set free.
My sin is GONE! It has been removed from me.
Lifted from my soul and life
and God has forgotten it ever happened.
I am washed. I am free. I am clean.

Unconditional forgiveness,
   needing no confession to make it true . . .
      but awaiting my repentance
         to make it mine.

THE SIN OF THE WORLD

The Lamb of God who takes
away the sin of the world!

It would be a mighty thing if I understood this fact for ME, for ALL my sins, but to understand that He took the sin of the world!

Until I understand this beyond 'me' – for those in my sphere, for others . . . and then for ALL people – I do not yet possess the power of the gospel, the Good News. Nor do I comprehend the heart of the Father-God as proven by His Sacrifice of the Lamb-Son.

THAT would be the change of my entire view
      of every person and every situation . . .
            present and past,
            and even of all humanity's history.

   "They" – all of them – are forgiven as well as me.
   ALL people are forgiven and altogether forgiven!

Those who know it, those who reject it,
even ones who never heard it.
Those who hate God, those who leave Him.
The heinous, the corrupt, the most evil.
All forgiven.

Incredible! The "sin of the world"
has been taken away.

Myriads will refuse that gift. Many will die covered in
their sins.

**A tragic waste, a needless hell, for
all sin has been whisked away . . . and vanished.**

*He has not dealt with us as our sins deserve
or repaid us according to our offenses.*

*For as high as the heavens are above the earth,
so great is His faithful love toward those who fear Him.*

*As far as the east is from the west,
so far has He removed our transgressions from us.*
Psalm 103:10-12 HCSB

The Legal Universe

To forgive is now a legal matter. This is how God has arranged it.

Forgive and the result is you are forgiven.
Refuse to forgive, break that law, and there is
      an inevitable consequence – to YOU,
      not only the offender.

The universe is a legal system. The entire universe operates by laws of nature sealed in place by God.

      All things in God's creation operate
            under their own laws,
            internal and external.
                  The laws of God run the universe.

Everything was created under laws of its operation, for the purpose God had in mind. Boundaries of function were given to every thing created.

The moon is confined to its orbit.
The fish are bound to life in the waters.
And so on . . .

LAW GOVERNS ALL

God's law is meticulous over all His works. The law given to Moses governed every phase of human life – relationships, works, even accidents – all matters had their law.

Justice and equity were the foundation of the Law given
to Moses.

The Hebrew nation was to operate within the confines of
precise ethics taught by God's law.

The Ten Commandments are the bedrock of the Law.
The moral laws of nations have been founded on this set
of simple but unbending laws that covered all aspects of
mankind's behavior.

**The Law issues from the nature of God and reveals
His very Being in its Fixed Purity.**

His character is perfect Holiness, an absolute Standard for
which compromise is not possible.

God's Law – issuing from His Holiness – was given
to humanity and recorded in Scripture, that we might
glimpse the nature of the Creator and how far we have
fallen from His presence and His pleasure.

The Cross is proof of the inflexibility
of God's holy law.

Sin, which is falling short of His Holy Law, required a
death penalty that only God's Pure Son could take. No
way around that death penalty.

Christ satisfied God's Law by His perfect life of
obedience. And He satisfied the justice of that Law in His
vicarious death, executed by the sentence of death my sin
earned for me.

From the womb,
every person earns the death penalty.

"Born in sin" by being born a sinner, from sinners.
Every person born . . . can only sin. For he *is* a sinner.

And especially are we blind to
our own prospects of execution.
"*They* deserve death.
Certainly not me."

Mere rebellion of an infant's rage sets up its courtroom of
guilt unto death. The universe is set on a legal basis. That
fact we must understand. Our concept of accountability
depends on it. Our commitment to forgiveness – our
primal need for forgiveness – rests on that understanding
of God's Absolute Justice.

Humanity is a criminal on the loose,
unaware of his own lawlessness,
believing his little misdeeds
are not that serious.
"God understands."

Many Christians believe that grace took away all the
law. That everything is all right because Christ lived as a
human being and understands our frailty.

Others live under the Old Covenant Law, already proven
impossible to fulfill.

GRACE AND LAW

Even the born-again believer can want grace to be this:
    "God overlooks our sins; God excuses all."

God does forgive, completely, but forgiveness
    is a principle that rests on
        Holy and Impartial Law.

Grace is neither the absence of Law
nor the negation of the Law
        but the completion of it finally – in Christ.

**Grace imparts the power to fulfill the law
by Christ's indwelling life.**

Forgiveness is not bypassing the Law of God. Forgiveness
is the satisfaction of His Law and it removes the imposing
of Divine Justice.
That was fulfilled in Christ.

Jesus took on Himself the Justice that you and I will
escape . . .
        IF we forgive others.

God cleared everything that separated Him from you and
you from Him. He gave you the righteousness of Christ
as a gift, the one essential to fellowship with God—His
very own holiness.

THE DAY OF ACCOUNTABILITY

The shadow of that Day falls over all the New Testament.

So then each one of us will give an account of himself to God.
Romans 14:12 NASB

That was written to Christians, not unbelievers . . .

Everyone will give an account. A solitary appearance
before the Infinite Holiness of God. A reckoning in utter
nakedness of the soul's secret history.

To be unaware of total accountability, even for a
Christian, is to live in danger and delusion. To tremble
at this inevitable prospect is spiritual health by virtue
of hearing His Word. To ignore it is insane. Such is the
greatness of God's forgiveness, and we dare not miss it.

Sin admitted and placed under the healing flow
of Christ's blood . . . these sins will be gone.
Vanished, erased from history.

Your forgiveness extended to others will determine your
own forgiveness from God. All will be exposed and set in
Precise Justice by the One who alone knows the
True Dealings of the unseen heart.

The fear of the Lord is the beginning of wisdom,
And the knowledge of the Holy One is understanding.
Proverbs 9:10 NASB

By our making God as we want Him to be, we have lost
the wisdom of fearing Him.

Your unforgiveness will cost you the grace and covering of your own sin.

It will constitute your spiritual loss forever and ever . . .

THE DANGER OF DELAYED FORGIVENESS

When angry, do not sin; do not ever let your wrath
(your exasperation, your fury or indignation)
last until the sun goes down.
Leave no [such] room or foothold for the devil
[give no opportunity to him].
Ephesians 4:26-27 AMPC

Tomorrow lies in God's Providence
over life and death.
Yet tomorrow is not assured to us.

And eternity stands as a sentinel before us
in the dealings of every day.

Forgiveness has to happen today. It must be quick, before the sun goes down. Why? Because unforgiveness today becomes Satan's prison of bitterness tomorrow.

This is how God orders His justice. To forgive is now a legal matter. Break that law and there is an inevitable consequence—
to YOU, not the offender.

*And blessed [joyful, spiritually favored]
is he who does not take offense at Me.
Luke 7:23 AMP*

So Great a Salvation

Matthew 6:9-15 NASB
Pray, then, in this way:
"Our Father who is in heaven,
Hallowed be Your name.
Your kingdom come.
Your will be done,
On earth as it is in heaven.
Give us this day our daily bread.
And forgive us our debts, as we also have forgiven our debtors.
And do not lead us into temptation, but deliver us from evil.
[For Yours is the kingdom and the power and the glory forever.
Amen."]

Wonderful gifts, for every need and all protection!
To receive it all, to enjoy the very right to its fullness,
there is one condition:

And forgive us our debts,
as we have forgiven our debtors
[letting go of both the wrong and the resentment].
Matthew 6:12 AMP

The Lord's Prayer is sequential, and the 1-2-3 order is unmistakable. It is a list of the Father's priorities and gifts, all conditional upon this one crux: forgiving others. Even after the amen, this crucial condition – without which you cannot claim protection from temptation nor deliverance from evil – is emphasized again.

To be sure we understand that forgiveness is
a life or death spiritual matter, the Lord Jesus repeats this
one command,
      a clear and unmistakable requirement
      for our own desperate need of forgiveness:

We must forgive or lose ourselves and God.

For if you forgive others their trespasses
[their reckless and willful sins],
your heavenly Father will also forgive you.
But if you do not forgive others
[nurturing your hurt and anger with the result
that it interferes with your relationship with God],
then your Father will not forgive your trespasses.
Matthew 6:14-15 AMP

Such a price Jesus paid for your forgiveness!
So great a gift the Father gave, His beloved Son.

For God so [greatly] loved and dearly prized the world,
that He [even] gave His one and only begotten Son.
John 3:16 AMP

You and I were saved by a Love so vast, so selfless . . . and
it rightfully demands of us
      a reception *of that Love* and
      a surrender to this gift *of Love!*

Such a small cost, to forgive others,
given the consequence.

For if the word spoken through angels proved unalterable,
and every transgression and disobedience
received a just penalty,
how will we escape if we neglect so great a salvation?
Hebrews 2:2-3a NASB

Let us not be those who fall short of and
"neglect so great a salvation."

MY UNFORGIVENESS HURTS ME!

We harbor the hate of unforgiveness to our own peril.

And that is our very motivation to forgive.
We forgive for our own sake.

In the heat of terrible hurt and injustice,
I have often said aloud,
"I will not lose my God over you,
I forgive you now!"

Be kind to one another, tenderhearted,
forgiving one another, as God in Christ forgave you.
Ephesians 4:32 ESV

To lose your connection with God by unforgiveness
is to lose your Self and the yet unlived
story of your life.

It is important to know
how big is God's pleasure and blessing
for those who forgive!

The Cross of Jesus

Gaze long and deep at Jesus on the Cross.

When you see the awful magnitude of your sin,
you will know the wondrous gift of forgiveness.
Then you will believe in HIM . . . and receive.

Jesus Paid It All

This is a lovely song I learned as a child and even then, though I didn't understand it, the words were sweet to my heart. Written by one who knew the vast scope of God's forgiveness —

> *Jesus paid it all.*
> *All to Him I owe.*
> *Sin had left a crimson stain*
> *He washed it white as snow.*
> (Elvina M. Hall, 1865)

The only problem is that the lovely song doesn't tell the full story, or picture for us His torture,
>   or show how gruesome was the Cross
>   that saved my very existence.

The heart of the gospel is Jesus' Cross
>   of unspeakable agony.
>   Look what it cost to give us
>   the utterly free gift of absolute, unending,
>   unstoppable forgiveness!

Maybe we need to know more about
>   the hideous price paid to buy us for Himself.

SEEING THE CROSS

I had read of a few believers who had seen the Cross by vision or by revelation. So I prayed fervently for some time to see the Cross in all its meaning and reality.

I wanted to know intimately what my Savior suffered and accomplished.

I made Paul's 'determined purpose' my own:

> *That I may so share His sufferings as to be continually transformed [in spirit into His likeness even] to His death.*
> Philippians 3:10b AMPC

I really thought that meant just living through His same life experiences with similar sufferings of rejection, slander, etc.

I was to learn that to share His sufferings had far more vivid implications. And how grateful I am!

To share in the fellowship of Christ's suffering *is* transforming.

SHOCKING SCENE

We were having an early morning prayer meeting in my home.
Suddenly I saw the Cross – fully vivid to my spirit. And I fell down to kneel at a bench, weeping.

I saw with horror that Jesus was not merely carrying our guilt, paying for our sins . . .

He was swallowing our death!
And the agony of that was darker and more horrible than words could describe.

The death that humanity earned was pouring into His body. Out of me came an involuntary scream, loud and piercing. It was unbearable to witness and with the scream, the scene began to fade from my spiritual sight.

Honestly, I don't remember what came next. I scarcely could consider how shaken the people there must have been, because I was in shock. Jennifer told me I couldn't speak for some 15 minutes, and I shivered so hard that they wrapped me in a blanket. We were all stunned and sat in silence for some time.

Finally all I could say to them was,
    "I saw that Jesus swallowed our death!
    It was the most terrible, horrifying thing.
    He didn't only take our sin."

I had always viewed the Cross as Jesus bearing our sins and that was enough for me. But I had never heard of this aspect of Jesus' suffering. The phrase 'swallowed death' was familiar and I found it later in one of Isaiah's prophecies about the Messiah.

*He will **swallow up death** [in victory;*
He will abolish death forever].
And the Lord God will wipe away tears from all faces;
and the reproach of His people He will take away
from off all the earth; for the Lord has spoken it.
Isaiah 25:8 AMPC (emphasis mine)

I came to understand that to swallow death was to take into Himself not only the sin of mankind, but the entire consequences of sin—the penalty of death, the very sentence of death for all humanity, of all time.

Jesus took into Himself the entire scope of sin,
its destruction, its punishment, and its final penalty:
absolute and eternal separation from God.

The most terrible destiny – unimaginable and inevitable
to all who remain sinners.

Death was *swallowed* by God's Son . . .
Who could take that in?

JESUS SWALLOWED DEATH

The vast death He took within led to Christ's most
excruciating agony of all, the utter darkness of separation
and rejection of God.

What should have been our rejection and separation,
our darkest death,
Jesus chose to swallow . . .
so that we need never know such horror.

*About the ninth hour Jesus cried out
with a loud [agonized] voice,
"ELI, ELI, LAMA SABACHTHANI?" THAT IS,
"MY GOD, MY GOD, WHY HAVE YOU FORSAKEN ME?"*

*And Jesus cried out again with a loud [agonized] voice,
and gave up His spirit [voluntarily, sovereignly dismissing
and releasing His spirit from His body
in submission to His Father's plan].
Matthew 27:46, 50 AMP*

Jesus could bear all the macabre suffering,
  but He could not survive the loss
   of His beloved Father.
    A loss that belonged to us . . .

In unimaginable torment,
  the Only Innocent Man died our just execution.

And in those moments of severed union,
  the Lamb took away the sin of the world.

  Jesus swallowed the whole of it, the terrible entire.

Some believe Jesus' heart literally burst.

  He abolished death forever.
  Yes, oh yes! Jesus paid it ALL!

Then, when our dying bodies have been transformed into bodies
that will never die, this Scripture will be fulfilled:
"Death is swallowed up in victory."
1 Corinthians 15:54 NLT (emphasis mine)

. . . Jesus, because of the suffering of death crowned
with glory and honor, so that by the grace of God
He might taste death for everyone.
Hebrews 2:9 NASB (emphasis mine)

Today Paradise

Two criminals were crucified with Jesus, one on either side.

One of the criminals who were hanged there
was hurling abuse at Him, saying,
"Are You not the Christ? Save Yourself and us!"
Luke 23:39 NASB

The other criminal had witnessed the crucifixion of Jesus firsthand and experienced his own terrible cross. He had heard Jesus declare this astonishing statement and the man must have marveled at such a thing:
"Father, forgive them, for
they know not what they do" (Lk. 23:34 ESV).

And of course Jesus' murderers were forgiven, right there.

But the other answered, and rebuking him said,
"Do you not even fear God, since you are under
the same sentence of condemnation?
And we indeed are suffering justly,
for we are receiving what we deserve for our deeds;
but this man has done nothing wrong."

And he was saying, "Jesus, remember me
when You come in Your kingdom!"

And He said to him, "Truly I say to you,
today you shall be with Me in Paradise."
Luke 23:39-43 NASB

PARADISE

Paradise is the place in heaven of the centrality of Christ.

> *. . . I will grant to eat of the tree of life*
> *which is in the Paradise of God."*
> Revelation 2:7 NASB

This man confessed his unworthiness, admitted his sin, and accepted his punishment. So he recognized the Man who was nailed beside him, experiencing the same agony as a criminal. He was indeed Jesus, "The King of the Jews," as Pilate's sign declared.

By humble and desperate asking, this thief, in spite of his deadly guilt, was instantly admitted into the highest, most privileged place in all the universe. Paradise!

> *To him who overcomes [the world*
> *through believing that Jesus is the Son of God],*
> *I will grant [the privilege]*
> *to eat [the fruit] from the tree of life,*
> *which is in the Paradise of God.*
> Revelation 2:7 AMP

The Tree of Life is Christ.
Jesus is the Life-center of the Garden of Eden.
He is the Lamb in the midst of Heaven's Throne.
Christ is the heart and nucleus of the universe!

And where He is, that criminal, that last-second convert,
    will be there in the presence of the King.

What God gave you is more than forgiveness.
He gave you *instant reconciliation* to Himself,
and a place in eternity in the very center
of His heavenly kingdom.

Only redeemed sinners will live in a forever Paradise.
And that is the inborn heart-dream of all humanity!

TWO CRIMINALS

Two criminals with the same guilt, both deserving a
sentence of death.

One scorned and hated the Man and demanded He prove
His Kingship.

The other confessed, and defended the Innocent King,
then humbly asked.
Just "remember me," but he never presumed
what he was given: Paradise.

Equal sin, same forgiveness for both criminals,
by the priceless blood
spilling out before their privileged eyes!

God has solved it all *for* all of us,
without any help *from* us.

But that divine gift of free will governs us.

It is eternally our choice . . . our knowing choice.

One man went to hell, the other to Paradise.
Our only two choices: heaven or hell.

THE ONE WHO WAS SAVED

This 'other man' is the permanent and stunning picture
of the mercy of God.

Our noble Savior was in the agony of His own murder,
swallowing the sin of all the world.
Yet He paused for one condemned sinner
and promised him (by unimaginable effort),

"Truly I say to you,
today you will be with Me in Paradise."
Luke 23:43 ESV

This is a perfect picture of repentance and the glorious
proof of redemption.

The man recognized Christ as King on the way to His
own Kingdom!

But the criminal on the other side hurled insults at Jesus,
same as the religious leaders and even the soldiers.

He who is not with Me
[once and for all on My side]
is against Me; and he who does not
[unequivocally] gather with Me scatters.
Matthew 12:30 AMP

TWO RESOLUTE CHOICES

Here were two men in the same state of guilt and punishment. But there were two different reactions to Jesus, and two diametrically opposite endings.

What was the difference between them?

First of all, both understood everything.
> Both men knew who this strange Man was:
> King and Messiah.

They both recognized His power to save them.

We know. We *always* know. Even if we fight the reality and deny it, we know.

The difference between the two men is not the blind versus the sighted.

The issue was profoundly simple and intrinsically basic.
> Each had a choice . . . the lie or the truth.

THE TRUTH . . .

One chose to live in the truth of his sin and also the justice of his punishment. This criminal had come to 'truth in the heart' – the awful reality about himself – and knew he was guilty without excuse.
> He freely admitted his guilt to the King and
> > admitted that he deserved to die for his sin.
> > > He had a deep moral reality . . .

Behold, You desire truth in the innermost being.
And in the hidden part You will make me know wisdom.
Psalm 51:6

He cried out to the King, but it was only this humble plea,
"*Remember me when You come into Your kingdom.*"

He had an uncommon hope in this King,
    to be saved from all he deserved,
    but he wouldn't have dreamed
    to be *with* this Man forever!
        Merely to be remembered . . .

And this repentant criminal went to Paradise
that very day – not just forgiven
    but completely redeemed and received,
    to live forever.
    For him, salvation was easy – just tell the truth.
        For the other criminal it was impossible!
        The Lie had become his hiding place
                and therefore his grave.

. . . OR THE LIE

The second criminal had the same opportunity, the same
knowledge. But he chose the lie. His sentence was 'unjust'
so he railed without fear against the Man he knew
was King on the cross next to him. He demanded the
right to be saved, without the reality of repentance and
confession.

This man knew everything: Who Jesus was and that He
had the power to save.
But he was full of delusion about his sin.
"I do not deserve to die."
And he turned all his rage on Jesus
for not doing what he demanded,
that Jesus save him – his way. NOW!

'My Way and Now' is always the dictate
of the sin-full man.

*One of the criminals who was suspended
kept up a railing at Him saying,
"Are you not the Christ (the Messiah)?
Rescue Yourself and us from death!"
Luke 23:39 AMPC*

He believed in the Lie as a way of avoiding the
consequences. He chose blindness because he wanted the
Lie.

He deliberately chose.

And we do choose. We fix on the death of the Lie or the
life of the Truth.

*. . . for their [moral] understanding is darkened
and their reasoning is clouded; [they are] alienated
and self-banished from the life of God [with no share in it;
this is] because of the [willful] ignorance and spiritual blindness
that is [deep-seated] within them, because of
the hardness and insensitivity of their heart.
Ephesians 4:18 AMP*

This profound verse defines the dark roots of loving the Lie. Willful ignorance! Which means deliberate choice.

> But the real root lies in the heart,
>> hardened by selfishness
>> and dulled by hate.

WE ALL CHOOSE

Our choice is always heaven or hell.

One man demanded to be excused, and he died.
The other humbly asked only to be remembered,
and he lived forever.

One man saw Jesus as existing only to be his ticket out.
The other saw Jesus as King with a coming Kingdom.

Such is the story of mankind.
We all know and we all choose.

> *And by unlimited seduction to evil and with all wicked*
> *deception for those who are perishing (going to perdition)*
> **because they did not welcome the Truth**
> *but refused to love it that they might be saved.*
> *2 Thessalonians 2:10 AMPC (emphasis mine)*

But why do most people *refuse to love the truth*?
The primal fundamental choice is about love.

Down in the core of our most secret being,
  we answer this question:
  How can I manage this life in which I find myself?

That primal choice is made very early in life, as early
as infancy. Lie or Truth is the value by which we live in
every place.

We instinctively build a coping system with life.
We decide how we will cope and what we will believe,
by a conscious decision between truth or lie.

And which we choose is actually *that which we love.*
  Self or God.

This love affair with the magic of lies can be changed
  but it rarely is.
  Even facing a death by intense suffering
  did not influence that one scornful criminal,
  though he hung on a cross beside God Himself!

The coming of the lawless one is by the activity of Satan
with all power and false signs and wonders,
and with all wicked deception for those who are perishing,
*because **they refused to love the truth** and so be saved.*

Therefore God sends them a strong delusion,
so that they may believe what is false, in order that
all may be condemned who did not believe the truth
but had pleasure in unrighteousness.
2 Thessalonians 2:9-12 ESV (emphasis mine)

Since God gave the gift of free choice,
>He will respect your choice,
>>even if it is to reject Him.

But know this,
>**each choice is ever and always
>heaven or hell, life or death.**

Who Murdered Jesus?

When Judas had eaten the bread,
Satan entered into him.
John 13:27 NLT

I prayed for a long time that God would let me see the
Cross, to understand what Jesus suffered and what
He achieved by that agony. One morning, I was again
praying alone for that experience, and suddenly I was in
the presence of the Cross.

No film or painting could capture what happened
at Calvary! I saw with the eyes of my heart that His
crucifixion was executed with the most gleeful savagery.

The crowd was not merely stirred to violence by the
religious. They were whipped into a bloodthirsty mania
for murder by the Murderer himself!

No dispassionate actions were present. Men were
carrying out Jesus' sentence with wild abandon, but Satan
was the monstrous force of hate operating through them.

Satan was the one who scourged Jesus,
the one instigating all the cruelty.
Satan was the scorner who taunted Him with contempt.
Satan was the cruel spear that pierced Jesus' heart,
even though He was already dead.

The devil could freely kill God at last and he went wild
with hideous pleasure to inflict the most gruesome
torture possible on Jesus. The scene was a madness of
fury and blood.

Truly 'all hell broke loose' on the Lamb . . .
                        and He took it all.

THE PROPHECY OF HIS SUFFERING

Isaiah saw the Crucified Lord,
        in the full horror of that sight,
                some 700 years before the Crucifixion.

> *Many people were shocked [astonished; appalled]*
>   *when they saw him.*
> *His appearance was so damaged [disfigured; marred]*
> *he did not look like a man; his form was so changed*
>   *they could barely tell he was human.*
>   *Isaiah 52:14 EXB*

Truly, Jesus is the Lamb slain
        "*before the foundation of the world*" (Rev. 13:8).

I didn't actually see Jesus in this scene specifically.
Who could bear that?

Never will we comprehend the horrific suffering of
                        His pure soul and His gentle spirit!

I simply knew with horror what was happening *to Him*.

Every aspect of His agony earned a particular forgiveness
for His followers.

May we gaze at this list that covers and clears away
every part of the huge weight of our sin.

*Yet He Himself **bore** our sicknesses,*
*and He **carried** our pains;*
but we in turn regarded Him stricken,
***struck down** by God, and afflicted.*
*But He was **pierced** because of our transgressions,*
***crushed** because of our iniquities;*
***punishment** for our peace was on Him,*
*and we are healed by His **wounds**.*

We all went astray like sheep;
we all have turned to our own way;
and the LORD *has **punished** Him*
*for the **iniquity** of us all.*

*He was **oppressed** and **afflicted**,*
yet He did not open His mouth.

***Like a lamb** led to the slaughter*
*and **like a sheep** silent before her shearers,*
He did not open His mouth.
Isaiah 53:4-7 HCSB (emphasis mine)

Above it all, the Cross was from God Himself . . .

Yet the LORD *was pleased to crush Him severely.*
Isaiah 53:10a HCSB

The LORD *says, "It was my will that he should suffer;*
his death was a sacrifice to bring forgiveness.
And so he will see his descendants; he will live a long life,
and through him my purpose will succeed.
Isaiah 53:10 GNT

"His death was a sacrifice to bring forgiveness."

You born-again believers are Christ's descendants, who receive the absolute forgiveness He suffered so to give you . . . freely.

For the first time, Satan murdered an innocent man. His death penalty was decreed and is waiting God's fullness of time for execution.

Then that lawless one will be revealed whom
the Lord will slay with the breath of His mouth
and bring to an end by the appearance of His coming.
2 Thessalonians 2:8 NASB

And we forgiven ones will watch with glee!

Priceless Blood

God paid a high price to save you to Himself.
If you can grasp it, you will see the treasure you are
in His eyes, as well as the costly gift of forgiveness.
The price for your freedom from sin and Satan was
something more valuable
than all the wealth on earth.

*For you know that you were not redeemed
from your useless [spiritually unproductive] way of life inherited
[by tradition] from your forefathers
with perishable things like silver and gold,
but [you were actually purchased] with precious blood,
like that of a [sacrificial] lamb unblemished and spotless,
the priceless blood of Christ.*
1 Peter 1:18-19 AMP

God sees you through the Blood of Christ and that blood
satisfied God's standard and God's principles. And He
is satisfied in you by the blood of His only begotten Son,
Jesus. The blood was shed for *you.*

*How much more, then, will the blood of Christ, who through
the eternal Spirit offered himself unblemished to God,
cleanse our consciences from acts that lead to death,
so that we may serve the living God!*
Hebrews 9:14 NIV

The blood of Christ washes us from the inside. We 'drink'
it by faith, without the need to comprehend the big HOW.
In mystery, the Holy Spirit enters us and applies the blood
of Christ to the innermost place of the conscience, and
there the blood washes away sin's darkness from the very
core of my being!

And guilt is gone for Ever.

The Blood of Christ is a baffling wonder that would fill volumes of description. The mystery of the Blood is beyond us, but the practical application is a matter of taking the scriptures and simply believing what is written about the Blood of Christ.

The Word is real and true,
more real than my mind can know
but true to my spirit in simple faith.
This is an eternal fact:

All things are cleansed with blood,
and without shedding of blood
there is no forgiveness.
Hebrews 9:22 NASB

Many ask for forgiveness with no consciousness of the Blood as the solution and *only source* of being forgiven. Never can we separate God's forgiveness from the Blood of Christ. Nor can we forget the Man who gave it.

The world would have a bloodless forgiveness
based only on God's goodness,
and so eliminate the very origin of mercy.

A bloodless forgiveness does not exist. Jesus' cup is the New Covenant **in His blood,** and when receiving His blood, we remember Him Who gave of that cleansing fountain!

Simply, as you drink the blood, 'Remember Me.' He asks just that of those who drink His blood.

May we faithfully remember and treasure
that sacred red stream that poured out
on the earth from His shredded body
and *took away the sins of the world.*

*In the same way He took the cup also after supper, saying,
"This cup is the new covenant in My blood;
do this, as often as you drink it, in remembrance of Me.*
1 Corinthians 11:25 NASB

THE GIFT SO FREELY GIVEN

In my earliest walk with the Lord, I found 1 John 1:9
and I was astonished. I had never heard that we could
be cleansed from sin; I expected only forgiveness. The
verse said that as I confessed a sin, at that moment I was
cleansed from that very sin. I was elated like a child!

*If we confess our sins,
He is faithful and righteous
to forgive us our sins and to
cleanse us from all unrighteousness.*
1 John 1:9 NASB

"Cleanse us from ALL unrighteousness!"

Oh joy, I would run to confess all my sins. So simple and
so perfect! I fully believed I was being cleansed of 'ALL
unrighteousness' because the Bible said so.

And it would be true.
Besetting sins began to just . . . be gone.

I would learn later that the cleansing I so treasured was actually from the Blood of Christ.

> *But if we walk in the Light as He Himself is in the Light,*
> *we have fellowship with one another,*
> *and **the blood of Jesus His Son cleanses us from all sin.***
> *1 John 1:7 NASB (emphasis mine)*

At the time I could barely believe that it was so easy
to be forgiven and
cleansed from all sin.

That was completely amazing to me!
I never dreaded seeing my many sins,
because I had the perfect cure in Jesus' Blood.

And those verses – 1 John 1:7-9 – became a 'prescription'
I have given many times
as a total solution to guilt.

That word was, and still is, my constant cure and God's faithful healing.

BLOOD OF THE COVENANT

A covenant is a contract between two parties. Each side makes an agreement.

The Old Testament covenant was this:

"If you obey Me then I will be your God."

Of course, no one in all the centuries could perfectly obey God.

Speaking of Israel, Paul wrote:

> *For they did not continue in my covenant, and*
> *so I showed no concern for them, declares the Lord.*
> *Hebrews 8:9b ESV*

Israel failed in their part of the covenant,
    so God was not obligated to perform His part.

At the Lord's Supper, Jesus served the wine and explained its meaning . . .

> *For this is My blood of the new covenant,*
> *which is shed for many for the remission of sins.*
> *Matthew 26:28 NKJV*

Jesus paid for sin, and also He took sin away.
But He went even beyond the issue of sin,
to establish a new contract between humanity and God.

It was a promise contract, and He guaranteed the promise with His own blood.

> *But as it is, Christ has obtained a ministry*
> *that is as much more excellent than the old*
> *as the covenant He mediates is better,*
> *since it is enacted on better promises.*
> *Hebrews 8:6 ESV*

In short form, this is the meaning of the New Covenant.

> "I, your God, **will do everything for you**,
>> from the inside out.
>> Your part of the contract is only to **believe**
>> that I will do what I promise."

For this is the covenant that I will make
with the house of Israel after those days, says the Lord:
I will put My laws in their mind
and write them on their hearts;
and I will be their God, and they shall be My people.

None of them shall teach his neighbor,
and none his brother, saying, 'Know the Lord,'
for all shall know Me,
from the least of them to the greatest of them.
For I will be merciful to their unrighteousness, and
their sins and their lawless deeds I will remember no more."
Hebrew 8:10-12 NKJV

The End of Satan

Your forgiveness is under siege.
War is declared against your freedom from sin and death.

You have an enemy who is out to defeat you,
    rob you of your own forgiveness,
    and separate you from the God who adores you.

A roaring lion is enraged that you can be freely forgiven
    and then exercise authority *over him!*

> *Behold I have given you authority*
> *to tread on serpents and scorpions,*
> *and over all the power of the enemy,*
> *and nothing shall hurt you.*
> *Luke 10:19 ESV*

The accuser harasses you day and night.
    A bombardment of lies intends to make you
    believe in your guilt instead of the innocence
    from your redemption.

Stay close to the Cross. Know the Cross.
The Cross of Jesus is your answer, your truth, and your
safety.

> *When He had disarmed the rulers and authorities*
> *[those supernatural forces of evil operating against us],*
> *He made a public example of them*
> *[exhibiting them as captives in His triumphal procession],*
> *having triumphed over them through the cross.*
> *Colossians 2:15 AMP*

Disarmed means "stripping away of weapons and hence the removal of authority and power" (Louw-Nida 49.20).

You can declare:
>"Satan, you were defeated
>on the Cross of Jesus Christ
>>and my sin is washed in Holy Blood."

You will have to fight to hold onto your forgiveness.
You will have to war against resentment.
You will have to do the only work, the work of believing.
And you will need to read the Truth
>and pray for the faith and revelation . . .

Jesus was nearing the Cross when He spoke this.

>*Now the judgment (crisis) of this world is coming on*
>*[sentence is now being passed on this world].*
>*Now the ruler (evil genius, prince) of this world*
>*shall be cast out (expelled).*
>*John 12:31 AMPC*

Do we know that Satan is an evil genius?

The most cunning attack on your life will come on the sacred ground of your forgiving and being forgiven. If the enemy can rob you there, you are destroyed for your destiny.

The enemy comes to remind you of your hurts and stoke the fire of your indignation. It is not you who thinks such thoughts. It is the enemy who tempts you to rehearse your offenses and doubt your forgiveness.

I have often realized, "Wait a minute, I have forgiven this person fully! This is the lie of the enemy!" Then I rebuke the enemy and say this rather silly but sincere statement: "Bring that up again and every time I will pray for 500 Chinese to be saved!" And I do! If you are not sure, just forgive again and pray for the one who wronged you. Otherwise, take your stand against the one who would constantly accuse you of unforgiveness.

Satan and his forces are not only defeated and disarmed. All the evil forces are 'expelled.'
He is not only powerless, he is cast out.
That's why he roams the earth to find a place to dwell in people. Give him no place, no welcome!

> *Be well balanced (temperate, sober of mind),*
> *be vigilant and cautious at all times;*
> *for that enemy of yours, the devil,*
> *roams around like a lion roaring [n fierce hunger],*
> *seeking someone to seize upon and devour.*
> *1 Peter 5:8 AMPC*

We are not fighting to win. The war is over. Our only 'fight' is to believe.

It is ours to believe and accept as FACT that Satan and all his supernatural forces of evil were defeated on the cross of Jesus Christ.

As a conquered foe, Satan has no weapons. Remember, he was "disarmed."

He can only hurl at you the **false accusation** that you are guilty. And you must stand on the FACT that by the Blood of Christ you are forgiven.

Satan can only **LIE** that he has power.

If you fear him, then you believe his lie. And you yourself will have given him his power.

> But if Satan has no weapons,
> then why does he seem so powerful?

We believers want to sail on a cloud of ease without trouble.

Accept it. This life in Christ is a divine school. It is not optional. There are tests and lessons. There is failure and correction. There is also reward and promotion.

The objective of this education is to know God
> personally and intimately,
> by living for and IN His will.

The lessons are not in a classroom of doctrine, but in the byways and trenches of real life. Search and ask for the object lesson before you. Find the solution by listening and searching and you will have passed the course and moved on in victory!

The school will be open as long as you live, ever learning that God is GOD. Truly. *Actually.* And the marvel is that He, your dear friend the Holy Spirit, is with you every step as your private Tutor and Advocate, your personal Wonderful Counselor.

The crucial lessons of this school will increase your wisdom daily.

He who is not [definitely on My side] is against Me,
and he who does not [definitely] gather with Me and My side
scatters.
Matthew 12:30 AMPC

Ever our lessons constitute a choice:
Who do you believe?

The issue is vibrant life or actual death.
What you listen to, you believe.
Who you hear, you follow.

Who will you listen to with your heart
and therefore . . . follow?

We learn to live by the FACTS of our Teacher's words. The
Bible is FACT, the only true reality. So our fight is about
faith in the facts so as not to be swayed by the dangers
and ordeals of a life under siege.

To experience all the joyous freedom of forgiveness,
you will come to live in the FACTS of Jesus' Cross victory
and His Blood's redemption.

It is a fight but this is a 'good fight' and worth all the
effort for its great reward.

We will fight the good fight how?

Fight the good fight of the faith.
Take hold of the eternal life to which you were called
and about which you made the good confession
in the presence of many witnesses.
1 Timothy 6:12 ESV

This is your life's greatest adventure:
>to believe and experience triumphant life,
>increasing in Jesus toward everlasting victory.

Christ has won the war and we get to live by His triumph, exist in His life, and rise above all that is under His name and beneath His feet.

Wherever He leads, we are surrounded with the triumph of Christ in every step.

>*But thanks be to God,*
>*who always leads us in triumph in Christ,*
>*and manifests through us the sweet aroma of*
>*the knowledge of Him in every place.*
>*2 Corinthians 2:14 NASB*

The Glory of the Cross

But God forbid that I should glory,
save in the cross of our Lord Jesus Christ,
by whom the world is crucified unto me,
and I unto the world.
Galatians 6:14 BRG

God is the Brooding Father to His children, knowing all their weak spots and unexposed sickness. He is in absolute control of what touches His growing children and is the Blessed Controller of their experiences and enemies.

Offenses and hurts are inevitable and deliberate. We define offenses as bad people, or instantly blame the devil. We need to know God, Who is behind it all.

His purpose IS the Son. All is for the Son. And all within us must be the Son.

God has now revealed to us his mysterious plan
regarding Christ, a plan to fulfill his own good pleasure.
And this is the plan:
At the right time, he will bring everything together
under the authority of Christ –
everything in heaven and on earth.
he makes everything work out according to his plan.
Ephesians 1:9-11b NLT (emphasis mine)

We are destined to play a part in that purpose and we are made ready by the Cross. God uses people and events and sufferings to conform us to Christ.

The Cross is living. It is the power and the principle for the Christian journey.

But we resist in ignorance of the level of our depravity, and by an arrogance that insists on living for God according to our own assessment.

> **So . . . the Cross of our solution**
> **comes in the form of the**
> **personal wrongs of daily confrontation.**

God sends the proud to expose my preening pride,
the evil to uncover my latent sins,
the angry to spark my fire of rage.

Offenses that bombard me are a frightful mirror,
forcing me to see the face I have not known.
And I ask forgiveness for attitudes that shock me,
things my Father knew all along.

What Has God Forgiven?

God has removed every obstacle between us
and provided for our entire need . . .
without any help *from us!*

What is Sin?

Who have I offended? Who?

David said in his confession,

> Against You—**You alone**—I have sinned
> and done this evil in Your sight.
> So You are right when You pass sentence;
> You are blameless when You judge.
> Psalm 51:4 HSCB (emphasis mine)

I can easily focus on who offended me.
But the question is Who have I offended?

David's prayer of repentance . . .
"Against You and You only have I sinned."

I always wondered – considering his sin – how it could be God only.

Then one morning in prayer, I saw!
It *is* God and only God I have offended.

All my sin and sins were against my perfectly wonderful Father!

This earth is His,
everything from a blade of grass
to the world of nations . . .
Because He created all things –

ALL belongs to God.

And every sin, whether commission or omission,
is ultimately against HIM.
Against Him!

The earth is the LORD's, and all it contains,
The world, and those who dwell in it.
Psalm 24:1 NASB

We crucified His Son.

His only Son, the treasure of His heart.
The object of His ardor.
The satisfaction of His purpose.

I sinned against my self.
I sinned against everyone I have loved
        and those I didn't love.
I sinned against the world and its authorities.
I have nothing but a record of sin . . .
        but it was all against *God!*
Aimed *at* Him, *because* of Him. *And He deserved none of it.*

**We hurt what belongs to God, that which He created,
and we kill what God loves.**

There was grief as I experienced this repentance from the
Holy Spirit. He strikes at the deepest root of your heart
        and exposes you to you, and worse . . . to GOD!

My heart was broken by what I had done to *Him* and to
what was *His.*

When I looked up, lying on my desk was a Bible,
  open to this passage
  (which I had not been reading):

But if the servant shall plainly say,
I love my master, my wife and my children; I will not go free.
Then his master shall bring him to God
[the judges as His agents];
he shall bring him to the door or doorpost and
shall pierce his ear with an awl; and he shall serve him for life.
Exodus 21:5-6 AMPC

I prayed this passage and asked anew to be His
bondslave. My ear belongs only to the Master.
  Who owns your ear has you.

I have been the prisoner of the Lord. He captured me to
places against my preference and put me where I would
die.

But a bondslave of the Lord is a volunteer to be HIS slave,
bound to Him without any choices or will of his own, no
escape . . . for life. By choice.

You should have the same attitude
toward one another that Christ Jesus had,
who though he existed in the form of God
did not regard equality with God
as something to be grasped, but emptied himself
by taking on the form of a slave,
by looking like other men,
and by sharing in human nature.
Philippians 2:5-7 NET

David committed terrible sins, yet he reached the deepest essence of true sin. His Psalm 51 confession is the perfect repentance.

> *Against thee, thee only, have I sinned,*
> *and done this evil in thy sight.*
> KJV

David was forgiven, redeemed, and made a star of God's love story.

This is the height and depth of sin . . .
and the measure of God's unfathomable forgiveness!

The Murder of God

God entered our human frailty and made Himself
vulnerable to our deepest evil. Jesus, innocent of any
offense against us, opened His arms and
     let us slaughter Him with all the vicious disdain
        of our primal hate.

Eden showed us that to refuse God is to hate God, and
next you murder your brother.
     The Tree of independence is a Tree of death.
     For one thing, the death of love.

Independence of God is the displacing of God . . . *as God.*
     As I lust to be god, I will hate God *for being God*
        instead of me.

**This is sin—it lies in the buried core of every heart—the
craving to murder God.**

We say, as though it was merely His duty and only His
idea (having nothing to do with us), "He died on the cross
to pay for our sins. How noble of Him. What price He
paid!" Yet that is not the full story. It is about Him, but
also about me.

That crucifixion story is very personal,
        grim and accusing . . .

Years ago, I began to pray fervently for a new realm of repentance by the revelation of the Spirit about my sin. Issues I didn't see, I wanted to see.

Finally the light hit and I saw sin, its true reality, for the first time.

IT WAS ME!

I was the one who murdered God because I secretly can hate Him. I can hate Him for no other offense than this: He is God and I am not.

"Jews plotted the murder of Jesus. The crowds killed Jesus. Roman soldiers killed Jesus.
It was 'they' who did it, but certainly not me."

No, give me sufficient pressure to the place of my fondest rights, give me enough fierce suffering, and I would come out with nail and whip to tear my own Creator to shreds by the most agonizing death I could effect.

Every person ever born could murder, with relish, the God who dreamed their being—
simply for that unmovable fact: He IS God.
And there is no Other!

WE ARE NOT INNOCENT

The thorns that punctured Jesus' scalp, dug into His skull and bloodied His hair . . . covered my arrogant sins of thinking, the independence of my opinions, and the cruelty of my judgments.

The lashes that ripped pieces of flesh and muscle from His bones . . . earned the healings that my sin has done to sicken and disturb my own body.

The beatings He didn't deserve should have been mine.
He took the punishment I will never suffer.

From head to foot, His blood gushed out of a thousand wounds and tears, cuts and holes from nails, a crude spear driven into His very heart.

The price He paid to secure my legal freedom, my total forgiveness! Only in wrenching repentance from God's Light can I comprehend even a miniscule speck of it.

Because I didn't know the depth of my own depravity,
I could not see the horror of His suffering . . .
because of me.

I am the one who mocked Him
and dared Him to defy my killing.
I took His last garments from His back
to gamble with my soul.

I killed Jesus.

"But I wasn't there!
　　Prove I would have killed Him.
　　　　It's not real to me."

To hate any person, made by God, is to hate Him,
including the hating of my "self" (1 John 4:20).

**Had the high priest not ordered it, I would have.
Had the soldiers failed to beat Him, I would have.
Had the centurion not driven the nails, I would have.**

Jesus knew the typical human thoughts of the Pharisee
hypocrites.

*You say, "If we had been living in the days of our fathers,
we would not have been partners with them
in shedding the blood of the prophets."*

*So you testify against yourselves,
that you are the sons of those who murdered the prophets.
Fill up then, the measure of the guilt of your fathers.*

*You serpents, you brood of vipers,
how will you escape the sentence of hell?
Matthew 23:30-33 NASB*

This is iniquity: to kill God and believe I am innocent.

"If we Christians had lived in Jesus' day we would not
have killed Him. 'They' did it. We are above the brutal
murder of God's Son. We Christians today are far too
civilized. Much too knowledgeable now."

By that secret patronizing, we give proof that we are the same vicious murderers who ripped His flesh from His bones, and loved His bloody agony. We too, by false innocence, "testify against ourselves" by the blindness to our guilt, by our superiority to 'those-lesser-than-us' who killed our Blessed Savior.

There dwells in every descendant of Adam the ambitious lust to be God and a madness of hatred because He is! We are – by very nature – killers. Cains are we.

> We murder by words, by deeds, by thoughts
> that boil and seethe
> in the angry cauldron
> of a primitive heart.

The heart is more deceitful than all else and is desperately sick;
Who can understand it?
I, the Lord, search the heart, I test the mind,
Even to give to each man according to his ways,
According to the results of his deeds.
Jeremiah 17:9-10 NASB

TO HATE IS TO MURDER

For God – who knows the hearts of men – considers that murder is an issue of the heart.

> Secret thoughts prove the potential
> and so it is guilt of the deed.

You are jealous and covet [what others have]
and your desires go unfulfilled;
[so] you become murderers.
[To hate is to murder
as far as your hearts are concerned.]
You burn with envy and anger
and are not able to obtain [the gratification,
the contentment, and the happiness that you seek],
so you fight and war.
James 4:2 AMPC (emphasis mine)

Hatred and greed prove we are simply assassins
without a corpse to prove it.
We are all a killer in the making,
having descended from myriad murderers.

We murder reputations, we kill relationships,
we annihilate confidence, we crush individuality,
we quench life and terminate the move of God.
We curse with thoughts and kill with words.
We plot to destroy.

Confident fools, certain we are right and even righteous
in our killing . . . just as 'they.' *"Doing God a service."* The
ancients killed the prophets because they were the closest
link to the God who kept interrupting their schemes to
rule.

We silence our 'prophet.'
We want to kill the Voice of God.

But God, who all along knew our murdering ambition, came in all the innocence of a lamb, laid Himself sweetly down and let us cut His throat. Man could finally do to God what he had before been able to do only to his brother . . . torture, maim and execute. Really – not figuratively, not in effigy! Actual murder. Unimaginable suffering.

> We longed for Him to be in agonized pain, to reject Him and have Him suffer for it.

All the vicious attacks of humanity were given to Christ . . . contempt, rejection, societal casting out, berating, mocking, beating—until the Son of God was so broken, so battered, that His wooden cross could not be borne on His bloodied shoulders.

Jesus died the absolute death of humanity's subconscious dream.

We rehearse it at Easter on the stage, in righteous horror as though we couldn't imagine "their" so hurting Him, our precious Jesus. We cry for Him but, "We were not there." At best we could say, "I was in the crowd." *NO.*

I held the whip that thrashed Him till His flesh hung in strips and white bones saw the sunlight. My spit ran down His face. "I" pulled out His beard and mocked His Name. I nailed huge spikes into His innocent hands and feet.

> I did it . . . because I could have.

To us, sin is just a painful collection of actions and
failures, a list of embarrassments. But sin is not plural.

Sin is singular.
> One sin – the hate and murder of God.
> All other sins tie back to that ONE.
> It is the origin and the reason.

> "Oh, my God, I killed You.
> By my bare hands I tore You to pieces
> with willful delight!"

This is the bottom, the bedrock of repentance.
> **This is sin. The ultimate sin. The root of all sin.**
> **To murder God . . .**

We blithely annihilate Jesus . . .

We exalt a mere human to His place
> and so disown Him.
We reduce Him to a little baby in a mother's lap
> and so reject the Real Man-King.
We hang Him on a dramatic cross
> and leave Him permanently dead.

When we say who He is and is not, we 'create' Him.
And by that arrogance, we destroy a personal God by
invalidation.

Oh, we have invented many ways to murder God.

We might see that we forsook Him as did all His followers. We might comprehend that we denied Him, as did Peter. We might even guess that we would have screamed for Barabbas. But to see that "I" was the one who murdered the Savior I proclaim and serve? That thought would rarely find us willing to consider.

Yet this is what He forgave:
His own undeserved murder.

But Jesus was saying, "Father, forgive them;
for they do not know what they are doing."
Luke 23:34 NASB

While Jesus hung dying of murder,
He forgave His killers.

This is what I have been forgiven.
Not merely stealing, lying, coveting and all the rest.
These are but symptoms of the Real Sin.

This is sin: to murder God.
Of that I am forgiven!

Jesus died to pay for His own murder
and I, the killer, am free.
He, my victim, took my death penalty!

My gratitude spills in endless tears on His feet,
forever gashed with nail holes.
Forgiven for my own murder of God!

My God, let me love You with the unfathomable love
You gave me on the Cross even as my hand was piercing
You. *I never knew I was the one who killed You!*

Still today, we do not know what we are doing.

Before I understood . . . long before I asked,
this is what You uttered in Your final fading strength:

> *Father, forgive them . . .*
> *Luke 12:34*

And the Father did forgive,
by the death of the Innocent for the guilty.

Perfect Forgiveness

YOU ARE FORGIVEN

Your sins are gone and not even remembered.
Your total forgiveness for every thought, word, and deed
gave you access to everything else that God has achieved
in the crucifixion of Jesus.

What God gave us by this extravagant gift of forgiveness,
is far beyond our highest dreams
and infinitely above our imagination.

YOU ARE RECONCILED

We were born separated from God.
The sin nature that we were born with
was the hindrance that separated us from God.

He graciously cleared every hindrance
that separated Him from you.
God came down to solve you entirely,
to remove every separation from Himself.

For if while we were enemies we were reconciled to God
through the death of His Son, it is much more [certain],
now that we are reconciled, that we shall be saved
(daily delivered from sin's dominion)
through His [resurrection] life.
Romans 5:10 AMPC

God made it possible for you to live forever,
                    to live knowing Him.

          God did it all, needing nothing from you.
          All was put on the Son of Man to rend the
          veil that separated us from the Father of Lights.

Through the Cross, you died with Christ and rose with
Him. God gave you complete reconciliation with Himself.

          There is nothing between you and the Lord.
                    If some shadow makes Him seem remote,
                    just ask and He will show you the problem.

Any sin He brings to light is instantly resolved
          because you are already reconciled to Him,
          by Him.

          But all things are from God, Who through Jesus Christ
          reconciled us to Himself [received us into favor,
          brought us into harmony with Himself] . . .
          2 Corinthians 5:18 AMPC

YOU ARE ADOPTED BY GOD

God decided in advance to adopt us into his own family
by bringing us to himself through Jesus Christ.
This is what he wanted to do, and
it gave him great pleasure.
Ephesians 1:5 NLT

Imagine this, picture this:
>God wanted you for Himself.
>To save you gave Him great pleasure!

The Lord Almighty bought you,
>purchased you out from hell, judgment and death
>to own you and enjoy you.
>>And you are meant to enjoy His enjoyment,
>>>every moment of your endless life.

We see God wrongly.
We don't see ourselves as being His delight.
We are too conscious of our familiar sin-self.

Just as a new baby is an utter joy, needing everything
from us and giving nothing to us, so God is, above all,
Our Father.

>He delights just in our existence and
>needs nothing from us for His joy.
>Delight is Love exultant.

Sometimes I experience God's delight in a person,
>some I know well, others I know only slightly,
>and there are those I know by name only.

>God's delight in us is something so exuberant
>as to be shocking.

In God's Beloved Son, YOU are a vessel of His delight,
created to enjoy His loving enjoyment of His children,
regardless of our past impurity,
> just based on His own good pleasure.

For God so [greatly] loved and dearly prized the world,
that He [even] gave His [One and] only begotten Son,
so that whoever believes and trusts in Him [as Savior]
shall not perish, but have eternal life.
John 3:16 AMP

YOU ARE A NEW BEING

Jesus took into Himself every human problem:
pain, despair, sin, regret, depression, sorrow, abuse,
scorn, lies, delusion, presumption, destruction, poison,
curses, judgment, rejection, abuse, abandonment,
sickness, violence, murder . . . and much more.

Jesus swallowed the devastation that is the outcome of
sin. In essence, He took you and me **out!** Right into the
grave with Him, the only solution for us wretches was
death. He took us sinners into His own death and died
Himself.

You have died . . .
Colossians 3:3 NASB

We have died with Christ . . .
Romans 6:8 NASB

You are solved because you are gone. And you are raised
to a new life with Him.

HOW? Mystery. Know the fact and you won't need to understand the how.

> This is an unchangeable fact.
> God said it and so it is so.

Your sin-filled self is actually dead with/in Christ and you have been recreated, all new . . .

God Almighty created for Himself a new YOU, a vastly different person than you, one that is capable of knowing Him, hearing Him, and even seeing Him. Your new YOU is wired to be like Christ and live as Him in the world.

> *For if a man is in Christ he becomes*
> *a new person altogether—*
> *the past is finished and gone,*
> *everything has become fresh and new.*
> *All this is God's doing, for he has reconciled us*
> *to himself through Jesus Christ; and*
> *he has made us agents of the reconciliation.*
> *2 Corinthians 5:17 PHILLIPS*

YOU CAN KNOW GOD INTIMATELY

From the Cross of God's love for this world and for you,
there is nothing more astonishing,
nothing more unimaginable and
certainly nothing more wonderful than this:
God gave Christ to dwell within His children!
In actual presence, in living reality.
The ultimate gift of God to humanity
is the indwelling presence of Christ.

He is the life you cannot live, the good you cannot be.
        He is the Love you don't possess,
        the Power in place of your weakness.
        Jesus IS the Forgiveness you cannot give.

Christ Jesus is all you are not
        and He takes you into His very being
                to be in Him as He is in you.

There is no greater intimacy than this: Jesus lives in you
and you in Him. You will learn Christ by watching Him
in action *through you!*

> *Abide in Me, and I in you.*
> *As the branch cannot bear fruit of itself unless*
> *it abides in the vine, so neither can you*
> *unless you abide in Me.*
> *John 15:4 NASB*

There is one plant. It is the vine Who is Christ and a
branch who is you.

        God made you one with Christ in the Cross.
                You are in Him and He is also in you.

        He will be patient where you cannot.
        He will be kind when you would not.
        He may very well be angry when you don't feel it.

He is altogether different than you imagine,
but you are being molded into His nature all the time,
                as you come to know Him . . .
                        from within.

And finally God will have many children like Jesus, who will think with His great and mighty thoughts, and live in His majestic life.

If you abide in Me, and My words abide in you,
ask whatever you wish, and it will be done for you.
John 15:7

The Lord's presence in our spirit is more to be desired than any life experience, more valuable than every wealth or love or joy this world could give.

Christ is the ultimate joy of the human heart.
And He is yours . . .

YOU ARE AN IMMORTAL BEING

For the wages of sin is death, but the free gift of God
[that is, His remarkable, overwhelming gift of grace
to believers] is eternal life in Christ Jesus our Lord.
Romans 6:23 AMP

Eternal life means the indestructible life
of Christ Jesus our Lord,
His very Life, divine and holy.
Our gift of His Life is from and in and through His Life,
and never apart from Him.

Eternal life *is* Christ. You will never die because He will never die. He has taken His born-again children into *that dynamic Life.*

As we live by faith that we are living IN Christ, attached as a branch to His wellspring of abundance, we will increasingly experience His triumphant life taking more and more possession of us.

We will increase in spiritual riches, in the appearance of the Kingdom of God, and even in physical prosperity.

> *The righteous man will flourish like the palm tree,*
> *He will grow like a cedar in Lebanon.*
> *Planted in the house of the Lord,*
> *They will flourish in the courts of our God.*
> *They will still yield fruit in old age;*
> *They shall be full of sap and very green,*
> *To declare that the Lord is upright;*
> *He is my rock, and there is no unrighteousness in Him.*
> *Psalm 92:12-15 NASB*

"Sap" means an upward surging of life, new and fresh. We should not dread old age or resist it. In whatever number, our days are precious and there is finished provision for all our days, whether few or many.

Christ was constituted our Priest . . .

> *. . . on the basis of the power of*
> *an endless and indestructible Life.*
> *Hebrews 7:16 AMPC*

That triumphant, unconquerable, everlasting Life is Eternal Life, and it is yours and mine by His death and resurrection.

How to lay hold of this Life?

This is eternal life: that they may know You,
the only true God, and the One You have sent—Jesus Christ.
John 17:3 HCSB

The key lies in the word "know."

My favorite definition of this "know" is from Louw-Nida
(27.18):

> "Know: to learn to know a person through
> direct personal experience, implying a
> continuity of relationship – to know, to
> become acquainted with, to be familiar
> with. As to John 17:3 it is important to avoid
> an expression which will mean merely 'to
> learn about.' Here the emphasis must be
> on the interpersonal relationship which is
> experienced."

By a surrendered relationship unto God
and in Christ Jesus, eternal life is
increasingly revealed and experienced.
By obedience and repentance, our fellowship
with God and His Son becomes
a vivid manifestation of that marvelous Life!

Simply put, God intends for His children to
actually experience His presence in this life
just by seeking to know the Godhead.

ALL THINGS

Forgiving and being forgiven, the foundation of God's redeemed world! And that great choice, standing always before us, will be the beginning or the end of our walk with Him Who *is* God.

The whole realm of forgiveness is a vast outpouring of God's mighty plan for His Son, and lavished on you and me . . . Yet that great IF stands before us.

IF you forgive, you will be forgiven. If not, you won't.

Heaven opens for the forgiver.

> *He who did not spare His own Son,*
> *but delivered Him over for us all,*
> *how will He not also with Him freely give us all things?*
> *Romans 8:32 NASB*

I pray that we will glimpse
the vast and astonishing Power of the Cross
to open for us those matchless,
limitless 'all things.'

So many believers live and die without seeing the scope and majesty of this Gift of God's forgiveness.

For many years now, I have seen with great grief that most – even sincere Christians – seem to take so lightly the weighty issue of forgiving.

How very few truly forgive and ask forgiveness!

The greatest tragedy would be to lose your rich destiny
               by needless bitterness or unnecessary guilt.

In our time, it is common to presume total forgiveness
without the need for repentance. But the scripture is clear.
Repentance comes first, and only then is forgiveness
obtained.

        Sins confessed from a contrite heart
              will experience lavish forgiveness
                 for those very sins.

God has given this vast, immeasurable redemption,
at the cost of Jesus' blood, crucifixion, and hideous death.

All to give us freely . . . His perfect forgiveness.

God's Longing to Forgive

From Eden's fall, our God has longed to forgive,
planned to forgive . . . with passion to save us.

FORGIVENESS IN THE PSALMS

Look upon my affliction and my trouble,
and forgive all my sins.
Psalm 25:18 NASB

Though we are overwhelmed by our sins,
You forgive them all.
Psalm 65:3 NLT

Help us, O God of our salvation!
Help us for the glory of Your name,
Save us and forgive our sins
for the honor of Your name.
Psalm 79:9 NLT

O, Lord, You are so good, so ready to forgive,
So full of unfailing love for
all who ask for your help.
Psalm 86:5 NLT

Bless the LORD, O my soul,
And forget none of His benefits;
Who pardons all your iniquities,
Who heals all your diseases;
Who redeems your life from the pit . . .
Psalm 103:2-4 NASB

But You offer forgiveness,
that we might learn to fear You.
Psalm 130:4 NLT

Humility is the Lamb

Christ's humility as God
to confine Himself to humanity . . .
    that is lowliness incomprehensible
    to a people glutted with haughty blindness.

Have this mind among yourselves,
which is yours in Christ Jesus,
who, though he was in the form of God,
did not count equality with God a thing to be grasped,
but emptied himself, by taking the form of a servant,
being born in the likeness of men.
Philippians 2:5-7 ESV

Lamb-meekness . . . by chosen helplessness.
Lamb-surrender . . . in Gethsemane.
Lamb-silence . . . before accusation.
Lamb-vulnerability . . . to violence.
Lamb-forgiveness . . . to His own murderers.

Only a Lamb disposition could take away the sins of the
world. Christ alone has no puffed-up nature of willful
sin.

His humility lives in me,
    and my only humility is surrender to Him,
        to let His Lamb-life have a vessel in me.

This is the humility that is capable of forgiving
heaps of hurt and wrong.

Christ's humility is the only humility.

Behold, the Lamb of God,
who takes away the sin of the world!

Repentance

Repentance is the first command of Jesus, "repentance for the forgiveness of sins."

This lavish, magnificent forgiveness of all sin waits only for you to SEE you need it!

To need forgiveness . . . that is repentance.

To Repent Is a Command

Repentance is the first command of Jesus.
Before He said, "Follow Me," He said, "Repent."

Only after He said, "Repent,"
did He say confess, forgive, obey and go.

Repentance is the key to everything of God.
      It opens the kingdom and the heavens.
        Above all, repentance enters behind the veil
                        to SEE GOD.

When God brings the mirror of repentance, it is His love
pursuing you. The exposure of the heart's sin is for the
sake of love. Repentance brings you to the need of God,
and if He exposes you to yourself, the reason and the
result is that you can receive the experience of God's love
personally.

John the Baptist came first with the call for repentance:
    "Repent, for the Kingdom of heaven is at hand."

Jesus was baptized by John the Baptist,
              and the Holy Spirit came upon Him.

Then He was led of the Spirit into the wilderness.
The devil left Him after He survived His wilderness
temptation.

When Jesus heard that John had been taken into custody,
He withdrew to Galilee and settled in Capernaum.
These events occurred and then . . .

From that time Jesus began to preach and say,
"Repent [change your inner self—your old way of thinking,
regret past sins, live your life in a way that
proves repentance; seek God's purpose for your life],
for the kingdom of heaven is at hand."
Matthew 4:17 AMP

This *Amplified Bible* translation is a perfect definition of repentance.

1. Repent [change your inner self]
The word repent in Greek means 'change your mind.' When you change your thinking you alter your will. Your thoughts create your choices and your choices, your life.

2. regret past sins
Repentance is God's personal exposure of *your sins,* from His point of view.

3. live your life in a way that proves repentance
A change of seeing equals a change of living. Only real repenting brings a transformed life.

4. seek God's purpose for your life
The Hebrew word for repent is 'to turn around.' Turn around and face toward God, and find the wonder of your purpose – Christ Himself.

5. for the kingdom of heaven is at hand
The reason for this is that 'the kingdom of heaven' is here and now!

The kingdom of heaven had come down to earth in this
plain, simple Man and only souls who repented could
recognize Him.

John the Baptist preached one sermon: "Repent."
The Spirit was powerfully present to bring people to
repentance in preparation for Jesus' appearing.
Great crowds came to repent!

The Pharisees and Sadducees also came for this popular
baptism but John knew they had not repented, so he
called them on it.

> "You brood of vipers, who warned you to
> flee from the wrath come?"

Repentance cannot be faked.
It is not a man-made act of religion
and it is altogether too naked for show.

Only through Spirit-given sorrow for sin can anyone
see and grasp their own utter depravity.

John the Baptist 'made ready the way of the Lord'
by preaching a fiery repentance,
and when he was taken out,
Jesus began to preach the same.

The message is crucial!
Repentance is a life-and-death matter.

THE FIRST COMMAND OF JESUS

"Repent, for the kingdom of heaven is at hand."

This is Jesus' first sermon, the one calling and command spoken to all humanity.

It is not a suggestion, nor an option. God requires all to repent of sin.

The first edict of Jesus was not 'Follow Me,'
    nor 'Go and tell it.'
        His first order was just "REPENT."

Repentance is the foundation of a life in Christ.

    "You cannot have a true viable faith
    without going through the constant process
    of repentance. It is basic; it is *foundational*.

    "Repentance is where you build your life in God . . .
    and where He builds His in you."
    (From my booklet, *Foundation of Repentance*)

To need forgiveness, that is repentance.
And it is the beginning and the undergirding of all else.

There is nothing without repentance,
    no salvation and no kingdom belonging,
        no eternity and . . . no forgiveness.

Before God brought the Cross of perfect salvation and absolute forgiveness, He had to bring an assault of Spirit-emblazoned repentance
   to the poor blindness of a fallen humanity.

So it is today . . .

I want to quote Oswald Chambers who understood genuine repentance like few.

> "'Am I prepared for Jesus' coming? Jesus
> cannot come as long as there is anything in
> the way either of goodness or badness. When
> He comes, am I prepared for Him to drag into
> the light every wrong thing I have done?' And
> 'every' is exactly what it is. It is just there that
> He comes. Wherever I know I'm unclean, He
> will put His feet. Wherever I think I am clean
> He will withdraw them.
>
> "Repentance does not bring the sense of sin,
> but a sense of unutterable unworthiness. When
> I repent I realize I'm utterly helpless.
> I know all through me that I'm not worthy even
> to bear his shoes. Have I repented like that?
> Or is there a lingering suggestion of standing
> up for myself? The reason God cannot come
> into my life is because I am not through into
> repentance."
> (*My Utmost for His Highest*, August 22)

This is a man who knows by experience the crucial gift of repentance!

Repentance is the door to God Himself! There, at the bottom of your sin, you meet God anew and He grows ever more precious. And we enjoy the freedom of His sanctifying grace.

Repentance is agonizing, but it is the dynamite that blows up our walls and destroys our barriers, and then we are brought into the very presence of God.

No Repentance, No Love

Luke 7:36-43 NASB
Now one of the Pharisees was requesting Him to dine with him,
and He entered the Pharisee's house
and reclined at the table.

And there was a woman in the city who was a sinner;
when she learned that He was reclining at the table in the
Pharisee's house, she brought an alabaster jar of perfume.

And standing behind Him at His feet, weeping, she began to
wet His feet with her tears, and kept wiping them with the hair
of her head, and kissing His feet and anointing them with the
perfume.

Now when the Pharisee who had invited him saw this,
he said to himself, "If this man were a prophet
He would know who and what sort of woman
this is who is touching Him, that she is a sinner."

And Jesus answered him, "Simon, I have something to say
to you. A moneylender had two debtors: one owed him five
hundred denarii and the other fifty.
When they were unable to pay,
he graciously forgave them both.
So which of them will love him more?"

Simon answered and said,
"I suppose the one whom he forgave more."
And He said to him, "You have judged correctly.

Simon viewed the situation in a manner that set him
above all others. Pride, by the name of Satan, despised the
liberating forgiveness of Jesus.

Because of Simon's proud blindness,
>   he did not believe that Jesus was God,
>   and worse, he doubted He was even a *prophet*.

The man who sees life in ways that are flattering to him,
>   will be blind to Christ
>   when He is sitting at his own table . . .

**The person who is sure he knows,
knows neither God nor himself.**

Man has his opinions, but God has His knowledge of all
hearts. The Lord heard the secret scorn of Simon's unsaid
thoughts. So He began to show Simon the reality of his
heart and the meaning of love.

> *Turning to the woman, He said to Simon,*
> *Do you see this woman? I entered your house;*
> *you gave Me no water for My feet,*
> *but she has wet My feet with her tears*
> *and wiped them with her hair (v. 44).*

In that day, a servant washed the feet of your visitors.
Israel is very dusty and dry, and the people wore sandals.
It was much more comfortable to have washed feet, and
not just for the sake of the clean house. It was really the
comfort of the guest that was the object.

This was mere common courtesy –
to either provide a servant to wash the feet of guests,
or if you didn't have that, at least you gave a bowl of
water so guests could wash their own feet.

So little did Simon value the Lord Jesus,
    God of the Universe, Creator of all that is,
that he didn't give Him a common, ordinary courtesy
you would extend to everyone who came to your home!

"You gave me no water."

The Lord Jesus begins to show Simon the truth of the
scene before him.
        Simon viewed himself as superior to Christ,
            having knowledge greater than His,
                and superior to the woman,
                whose sin was so obvious to all.

Simon was the lowest one in the room . . .
but he thought he was the most religious
and the only one who really understood.

Jesus said,
    "You gave me no kiss, but she, since I came in,
        has not ceased kissing my feet."

It was a custom to kiss your guest. Men kissed men.
That is an oriental custom – one cheek and then the other.

If you didn't kiss your guest, it was an insult that said,
    "You are really a nobody.
    I have no esteem for you."

This sinful woman didn't kiss Jesus' cheeks or His head.
She kissed His dirty feet.
And she provided out of her own tears
    the water that was lacking
        through the contempt of Simon.

Then Jesus continued:

> *"You did not anoint My head with oil*
> *but she anointed My feet with perfume."*

Perfume was more costly than oil. The Lord Jesus said, in effect, "The most basic, ordinary courtesy, you didn't do because you don't love." How we behave will always give away the measure of our love. It always will.

You will always act on love . . .
or fail to act for *lack* of love.

No water, no service, no kiss, no affection, no oil, no perfume – no love.

The reason Simon was utterly blind to Jesus, to the humble woman, and above all, to himself? Simon had no deep experience of God-given repentance, no confession, and no asking God's forgiveness. As a result, he had no love for Christ.

Jesus concluded:

> *"For this reason I say to you, her sins,*
> *which are many, have been forgiven,*
> *for she loved much;*
> *but he who is forgiven little, loves little."*
> *Then He said to her:*
> *"Your sins have been forgiven."*
> *Luke 7:47-48 NASB*

(This concludes an excerpt from my booklet, *Seeing Him*.)

SEEING THE LORD THROUGH REPENTANCE

But whenever a person turns [in repentance] to the Lord,
the veil is stripped off and taken away.
Now the Lord is the Spirit, and where the Spirit of the Lord is,
there is liberty (emancipation from bondage, freedom).
And all of us, as with unveiled face,
[because we] continued to behold [in the Word of God]
as in a mirror the glory of the Lord,
are constantly being transfigured into His very own image
in ever increasing splendor and
from one degree of glory to another;
[for this comes] from the Lord [Who is] the Spirit.
2 Corinthians 3:16-18 AMPC

The veil is an impediment – the blindness of humanity's state of being until we turn to Jesus for simple help. This woman must have done so. When you simply change your focus toward Jesus, Light dissolves your blindness and you begin to see. And what you see first is your sin.

This True story must be your story.

There is only one Way to God: through Christ and His Blood of forgiveness.

Jesus said to him, I am the way, and the truth, and the life;
no one comes to the Father but through Me.
John 14:6 NASB

We get to the Father through Jesus' Cross. The way is repentance.

This woman, a known sinner,
>   is utterly transformed by Christ . . .
>   freed of shame, liberated of fear,
>   cleansed of guilt and even regret.
She is known, accepted, and Loved for the very first time.

She cares not how she appears nor how she is judged. She
has no more interest in herself – nor in any other person.
She is free of the world and of her own dark self!
With passionate abandon she sprawls before Jesus and
pours her happy tears and her treasures on His precious
feet.

She has *seen and received* from Jesus what no one else in
the room can see or understand!
>   God's love in Christ has been poured into her
>   personally, experientially.

> *We love, because He first loved us.*
> *1 John 4:19 NASB*

To such a One Who sets us free, welcomes us as though
we are pure and precious, we abandon all reserve.
We love Jesus' Love enough to *want to die for Him.*

By His gracious forgiveness, we are filled with love and
gratitude for the gift of cleansing, the peace that comes
from reconciliation to the Father.

Repentance is the door to the heavens
>   and the gateway to Christ.
Repentance is the way of change
>   from selfish pride to humility and love.

Repentance is the Light from above that dissolves the veiled delusion of our willful blindness. We see our awful self . . . then we see God – because we can.

Repentance gains all the freedoms and glories for which Jesus suffered so!

Repentance is the secret of Loving God.

To be forgiven is to Love the Forgiver.
We humans don't begin with Loving God. We begin with repentance and then we experience *His* love first.
We love by response,
        by being shocked into the Love of God.

The measure of repentance will be the size of our love for God. We receive His merciful Love and then we love Him with that Love.

When love for God is lavish and grateful, repentance is the explanation.

Repentance is a sword of Truth-in-Reality that pierces your heart and kills the inborn delusion that darkness is light and light, darkness.

The Word of death is also the sword of Life,
        leaving you cleansed by the Blood
        and healed by forgiveness.

The pure in heart are blessed, for they will see God.
Matthew 5:8 HCSB

Repent is not the command of an angry God.
It is the invitation of a satisfied Father:
"I have opened the way. Come to Me!"

The Way is made possible by the Cross of Jesus' sacrifice.

God has solved the entire sin problem, but we have to
need and receive His only solution. Ever we are free to
turn down freedom and reject forgiveness by refusing
repentance.

AT HIS FEET

As I write this, I realize that I am that forgiven woman at
His feet.

When I was 26 or so, I was a woman who had all her
dreams. I married my prince, a Naval Officer. I had three
perfect babies and a little brick cottage. On my knees
I had asked God for all these things and He had given
every one. I was a churchgoer merely by obligatory
habit. That's what you do in the South. You go to church,
whether God is there or not.

I had no problems. But suddenly I was feeling . . . not full,
as I should, but terribly empty. This was my song: 'Is this
all there is?' I felt guilty for being unfulfilled. I berated
myself, "Fool, what would it take to make you happy?"
I thought the issue was happiness. And I knew that if I
were Queen of England it would not be enough for me.

I felt I was a wretch for such selfishness. That was my own diagnosis. I did not know the word repentance, and I didn't comprehend that I was experiencing the Spotlight of God piercing to the depths of my heart.

I thought a bit about God. I had experienced Him as a teenager. Yet somehow, I had to know He was enough for my adult dilemma, and those experiences were not enough. I sank lower into what I thought was despair, the unwarranted unhappiness for which I felt so guilty. "Any woman would swap places with me," I thought. I was miserable about myself.

I began to feel I was not as good as I had believed. It came to me that I was a selfish mother and I agreed. Then it occurred to me I wasn't a nice person, as I had always believed. It seemed the more I saw myself, the more hopeless I felt.

I began to wonder if Jesus could be the answer. I felt that I had to know if Jesus was Who He said He was. If not, there was nothing to do but just survive your life until you die.

I would stand at the window of my beautiful little peach nursery and cry and cry. I knew there was no hope for me. It wasn't as if I could have a better life, I had the best! I knew there was nothing better. I began to ask God to help me, "If You are there."

No one in church appeared to know God. I looked into faces, searching for a glow that I believed would be there if you really knew God. No one in my circle of friends appeared to know God in a real way. I never saw one radiant face.

I listened intently and even desperately to the Episcopal priest for any mention of the name of Jesus. By this time, I knew my only hope was God. But the priest spoke only about doing good. He never spoke of Jesus . . .

Then it seemed a banner appeared over me. These words were always before me: "Thou shalt love the Lord thy God with all thy heart . . ." I said to God, "I don't love You. I don't even know You." And that meant a deeper hopelessness. If God wanted me to Love Him, then I was truly sunk.

It was Easter season and the priest asked me to speak to the ladies' group. I said yes, but I was totally unqualified to speak about God or Easter. I thought, "Well, I need to know how Jesus spent His last 40 days before He died." So I set out to study.

I pulled out my teenage Bible and began to read—Matthew, Mark, Luke, and John. I read for hours between diapers and meals. I would get to the end and start over again. Somehow Jesus rose from those pages and became alive to me. He was as real as a living person. And all that He said in the scripture was like a blaze to my heart.

On that Easter Sunday, a tiny French woman sang "The Holy City" and the words of the song told the story of the cross and resurrection.

> *The sun grew dark with mystery,*
> *The morn was cold and chill,*
> *As the shadow of a cross arose*
> *Upon a lonely hill.*

Jerusalem! Jerusalem!
Hark! How the angels sing,
Hosanna in the highest!
Hosanna to your King!
(Frederic Weatherly, 1892)

And suddenly God was there! I was so full I felt I could have burst into tears or shouted. God's love was flowing through my body and I was overwhelmed by His presence. All I could do was cry, I could barely contain myself.

In the months that followed I lived in a state of bliss. Jesus was so present I needed no one and nothing else. At last I was deeply satisfied and more . . . overflowing with the love of God.

I didn't know Christian words. It was a long time before I understood that I had experienced repentance by the Holy Spirit and forgiveness through Jesus Christ.

Later I discovered what happened to me in John 14.

*"Whoever has my commandments and keeps them, he it is who loves me. And he who loves me will **be loved by my Father**, and I will love him and **manifest myself to him.**"*

*Jesus answered him, "If anyone loves me, he will keep my word, and **my Father will love him**, and we will come to him and **make our home with him.***
John 14:21-23 ESV[1] (emphasis mine)

I had obeyed that one command, "Repent."

The more I repented, the more sorrow I felt and the more sin I realized and admitted without excuse or resistance. This agony went on for many weeks.

God's forgiveness began to open the heavens. Jesus was revealed to me through the Bible, and He was knowable. I saw Him! I knew Him!
> And the love of the Father
> flooded my whole being.

This is why I love repentance, why I always ask for it.
> It is the doorway to seeing God,
> as He reveals Himself!

O, Lord, You are so good, so ready to forgive,
So full of unfailing love for all who ask for your help.
Psalm 86:5 NLT

---

[1] In the Greek, *manifest* means cause to be seen, make known, to appear, be seen openly (Strong's #1718). *Home* means a place where one may remain or dwell (Strong's #3438).

A Broken Heart for Sin

In the Old Testament, David was one whose sin was great. When he began to see that sin in the light of God, he wrote the magnificent Psalm 51, the pattern for all time of true repentance acceptable to God. And it appears that God granted his every request.

His prayer was a cry of deepest sorrow:

> *Create in me a clean heart, O God,*
> *and renew a right spirit within me.*
> *Psalm 51:10 ESV*

Such was David's remorse that his heart was utterly broken.

By that heart anguish, he came to understand what God wants in repentance:

> *The sacrifices of God are a broken spirit;*
> *A broken and contrite heart O God, you will not despise.*
> *Psalm 51:17 ESV*

David's broken and contrite heart was the only sacrifice he could give to God, and such was His pleasure in the man's repentance that God used this to declare the mercies of the New Everlasting Covenant.

> *I will make an everlasting covenant or **league with you,***
> *even the sure mercy (kindness, goodwill, and compassion)*
> *promised to David.*
> *Isaiah 55:3b AMPC*

The mercy that David received in response to his total repentance was a restoration of his divine destiny, which was the throne of David, the type of Christ as King.

David was lavished with more than forgiveness. He was given love, compassion, kindness and goodwill. The record of David's sin, the Lord has removed and forgotten.

> *And when He had removed him,*
> *He raised up for them David as king,*
> *to whom also He gave testimony and said,*
> *'I have found David the son of Jesse,*
> *a man after My own heart, who will do all My will.'*
> Acts 13:22 NKJV

The "sure mercies of David" were perfect reconciliation with God, and then an entire restoration to the man's divine destiny, his eternal place.

The Throne of David is the Throne of Christ (Isaiah 9).

The same "sure mercies" are given to us who repent to the place of a broken and humble heart.

This is the incredible grace given through the Everlasting Covenant (Hebrews 8).

> *And that He raised Him from the dead,*
> *no more to return to corruption,*
> *He has spoken thus:*
> **"I will give you the sure mercies of David."**
> *Acts 13:34 NKJV (emphasis mine)*

The same vast and certain mercies of God
                    are mine and yours!

Grant us, Lord, the heart-wrenching depth of repentance
that opens Your own heart to us.

Repentance Lost

In the Old Testament, the penalty was according to the action.

Now in light of the Cross and the new 'Law of the Spirit of Life,'
**the crime of thought is equal to
the guilt of the act.**

*"You have heard that it was said,
'You shall not commit adultery.'
But I say to you that everyone
who looks at a woman with lustful intent
has already committed adultery with her in his heart.
Matthew 5:27-28 ESV*

*"You have heard that it was said to those of old,
'You shall not murder;
and whoever murders will be liable to judgment.'
But I say to you that everyone who is angry with his brother
will be liable to judgment;
Matthew 5:21-22a ESV*

*Everyone who hates (works against) his brother [in Christ]
is [at heart] a murderer [by God's standards]; and
you know that no murderer has eternal life abiding in him.
1 John 3:15 AMP*

Repentance is an act of grace, given by the mercy of God through the Holy Spirit to those who are in the posture of *receiving* grace.

God's condition for His mercy is very simple (James 4:6):

> ***God opposes the proud,***
> ***but gives grace to the humble.***

The word 'opposes' is too mild actually. The word in Greek means 'to set an army in array against, to set oneself in opposition to or in array against' (Strong's #498).

God is at war with pride, set in military array, ever ready to strike and defeat.

Grace is 'unmerited favor,' but the word means more than this can express. Grace in the original Greek is "that which causes joy, pleasure, gratification, favor, acceptance; the absolutely free expression of the loving kindness of God to men; the bounty and benevolence of the Giver; unearned and unmerited favor" (Strong's #5485).

Jesus' sacrifice gained us the favor with God that we could never have earned, such is the depravity of humanity. But grace is not given to all people. We must be in a heart attitude of meekness and humility, that is where grace is given lavishly.

Repentance is a gift of grace and will not come to the proud. A humbling has to happen first before repentance.

A PLACE OF LOST REPENTANCE

Here is a man who came to a place where repentance was lost to him.

Looking carefully lest anyone fall short of the grace of God;
lest any root of bitterness springing up cause trouble,
and by this many become defiled;
lest there be any fornicator or profane person like Esau,
who for one morsel of food sold his birthright.
For you know that afterward,
when he wanted to inherit the blessing,
he was rejected, for he found no place for repentance,
though he sought it diligently with tears.
Hebrews 12:15-17 NKJV

Esau understandably responded to his brother's trickery with rage. But then Esau went to such pride and fury that he fully intended to murder his brother. And Jacob escaped with his life only because his mother told him, and then arranged his flight from Esau.

So Esau hated Jacob because of the blessing
with which his father blessed him,
and Esau said in his heart,
"The days of mourning for my father are at hand;
then I will kill my brother Jacob."
Genesis 27:41 NKJV

Murder, in thought and intent, is the ultimate rebellion that invites satanic possession.

A murderous posture is the pride that says, "I am above the Most High God. I will take into my own hands what belongs to God alone: to decide life or death."

> *Everyone who hates his brother is a murderer,*
> *and you know that no murderer has*
> *eternal life abiding in him.*
> *1 John 3:15 ESV*

I have known those who are so filled with hate and bitterness that they will admit to actually rehearsing violent and brutal murder in their secret thoughts. Others have dreams of murder without any emotion of shock.

This rehearsed murder is focused not on the parent or the party that offended them, but on innocent people, even on their spouse and children, especially God's children. This is a very abnormal place, for these who go that far in thoughts of murder seem to have no remorse, much less repentance.

Every person who admitted such thoughts to me also claimed to be an authentic Christian. To meet any one of them, you would never guess the evil intentions of their hearts. It is very real that there are truly 'wolves in sheep's clothing' among us, just as Jesus warns. Murder is a Being and he ever searches for vessels who will receive his plans to kill God and take his place.

> *Be serious! Be alert!*
> *Your adversary the Devil is prowling around*
> *like a roaring lion, looking for anyone he can devour.*
> *1 Peter 5:8 HCSB*

I have come to believe that when you cross a line to secretly imagine and rehearse brutal murders, you have earned God's judgment as an actual murderer in that place of such evil. Satanic pride has taken possession and there is no humility, so no possibility to find a place of repentance (Matthew 5:21).

This is what can happen to anyone who is too arrogant to repent and too bitter to forgive.

Above all assaults, Satan wants to destroy
God's children by preventing forgiveness
and inciting bitterness.

**Satan gets a foothold when we pet anger
and wait too long to forgive.
This is why to forgive is a life or death matter.**

*The Lord will rescue me from every evil assault,
and He will bring me safely into His heavenly kingdom;
to Him be the glory forever and ever! Amen.
2 Timothy 4:18 AMP*

Chastened by Love

Offenses and hurts are inevitable and deliberate.
We define offenses as bad people, or instantly blame the
devil. But we need to know Who is behind them, for He
has a purpose.

The Cross is living. It is the power and the principle for
the Christian journey.

A JOURNAL OF UNCOMMON JOY

I love You, Lord—I dance and worship YOU for what You
have allowed to come into my life.

I love You, God Almighty, for what You have sent to
pierce, humiliate, torture, disappoint, and offend "THE
BIG ME."

I adore You for my murder!

You humiliated me in the place of honor I sought. You
destroyed me in the eyes of those I admired.

You bolted the door against my knocking. You blocked
the path of my insistence.
> You! It was You . . . all along. My Beloved.

In doing so, You came to kill my ambition and arrogance,
> my desire for the approval of man,
> my lust for acclaim.

You have fiercely, violently – as a Jealous Lover –
destroyed my pillows of comfort,
my caverns of hiding, my safe harbors,
my vile altars and . . . my own throne.

The offenses over which I stumbled . . . were the sword of
Your severing, freeing my heart from the prisons of my
putrid affections.

With every violent swing of Your sword, You set me
free – not of my dreams, as I believed, but of my chains.

You have given me, through injustice, slander,
        pain and persecution,
              my heart's desire: to belong only to You.

My thirst for You was hindered by my inability – no, my
unwillingness – to let go. Your Love, "cruel as the grave,"
did it for me (Song 8:6).

I adore You for Your Brutal Love, Your relentless fight for
my affections. Your capture of my heart-loves above all
other loves . . . lands, things, and people.

I fall before the Beautiful Feet that have trodden the very
soul of my being, ever pressing me into wine, flavored
for Your tasting. Drink, my Lovely Lord, of Your crushed
FRUIT.

**I kiss those Merciless Feet with tears of gratitude
for the tramping of my idols . . .**

You love me! You do so love me!

Every wrong, every humiliation was a blow from
Your Saving Love,
Your Blaze of Jealousy,
Your Unbending Demand of all my love.

You have fought ME . . . for me.

You have used my enemies – and my friends! – to crush
my soul and effect my release.

Yours is the Hand that Joseph finally saw, hidden behind
the cruelty of his murderous brothers, and the injustice of
his imprisonment.

Your Sovereign Hand crushed Joseph through the wrongs
You allowed (and even authored).
All along, Your Skillful Fingers were molding him into
readiness for a place of reigning,
a prosperity of riches, a position of honor,
and . . . an eternal significance.

And so You are doing to me. To all of us.

*For they (fathers) disciplined us for a short time
based on what seemed good to them,
but He does it for our benefit, so that we can share His holiness.
No discipline seems enjoyable at the time, but painful.
Later on, however, it yields the fruit of peace and righteousness
to those who have been trained by it.*

*Therefore strengthen your tired hands and weakened knees,
and make straight paths for your feet,
so that what is lame may not be dislocated but healed instead.
Hebrews 12:10-13 HCSB*

Foundation of Forgiveness

Forgiveness is letting go . . . to God,
and leaving your self to His defense alone.

Forgiveness Is

Forgiveness is . . . accepting God's sovereign use of people and situations to strip you of self-importance and humiliate your self-love.

Forgiveness is . . . faith in God's Controlling Permission and All-knowing Goodness pouring out toward tiny you.

Forgiveness is . . . hope that you will meet only Divine Mercy for yourself.

Forgiveness is . . . love for the Great Forgiver and simple obedience for His sake.

Forgiving is . . . letting God be God! And doing whatever He likes — or doesn't.

Forgiveness is *not* . . . a cowardly tolerance of evil.

Forgiveness is *not* . . . being "good" because that is the command.

Forgiveness is *not* . . . excusing the wrong by pity.

Forgiveness is *not* . . . explaining why, for there is never an explanation.

Offenses are sin. Period.
>Sin is not an "Oops, I didn't mean to."
>Sin is deliberate,
>>always a highly calculated choice,
>>>even if very unconscious.

What we do, we meant to do.
What we say, lives long in secret before
      it curses and hurts.
There is no 'why' for anyone.

        We are all "without excuse."

Forgiveness is *not* . . . swallowing the pain and lying to
yourself about its existence.

Such false forgiveness becomes blind-bitterness . . .
      buried and festering
         in deep unconscious sickness of soul.

It is dangerous because it becomes a contagious disease,
      hidden under the blankets of self-satisfaction –
      evil, ever spreading through words and deeds
      that cover and hide it.

Unforgiveness:
unacknowledged, unconfessed,
deadly to you and
highly dangerous to others.

The First Forgiveness

There is a fundamental, first-forgiveness, without which
no one will ever see their destiny or the face of Christ and
very likely will not live out their appointed days.

In our human tendency, this primal forgiveness is often
ignored because we unconsciously believe it's an offense
that doesn't deserve forgiveness.

It is the nature of all humanity to consider that we are
better than our parents. We could have done better, we
would have been more loving—on and on we compare
and rate ourselves superior. We believe, "Our Parents
failed to an inexcusable degree."

It is the first stronghold of pride and it is deadly . . .
to life and destiny, to health and spirituality. What we
don't realize is that to hate parents is to hate God.

From the beginning of time,
    He chose and orchestrated and planned
        the perfect parents for our story –
        but never ideal. There is no such thing.

God is building a story of His own Father-love and
family-redemption, but most people don't solve their
family dilemma enough to live out their special story.

If you are not satisfied with the parents God chose,
you will never be satisfied with anything or anyone
in this life.

All parents must be forgiven by their children.
No parent is perfect.
No family is flawless.

This fundamental forgiveness is for some a huge
forgiveness, but if you set up in your heart thoughts of
superiority to parents, things will not go well for you.

> *"Honor (respect, obey, care for) your father and your mother,*
> *so that your days may be prolonged*
> *in the land the LORD your God gives you.*
> *Exodus 20:12 AMP*

The Pharisees demanded that Jesus' disciples keep
the law of washing hands. Jesus' answer accused the
Pharisees of a much worse offense, to which they were
blind. They were not obeying God's fundamental law
about parents.

Then He added the frightening penalty of death.

> *He replied to them,*
> *"Why also do you violate the commandment of God*
> *for the sake of your tradition [handed down by the elders]?*
>
> *For God said [through Moses],*
> *'HONOR YOUR FATHER AND MOTHER,'*
> *AND, 'HE WHO SPEAKS EVIL OF OR INSULTS*
> *OR TREATS IMPROPERLY FATHER OR MOTHER*
> *IS TO BE PUT TO DEATH.'*
> *Matthew 15:3-4 AMP*

I wonder how many people die prematurely
by unforgiveness of the parents God chose.

I wonder how many of us find
that 'life doesn't go well with us,'
when the issue behind it all
is the failure to honor parents.

We would never dream that this is a matter of life or
death and quality of life.

Honor your father and mother,
which is the first commandment with a promise,
so that it may go well with you
and that you may have a long life in the land.
Ephesians 6:2-3 HCSB
(quoting Exodus 20:12)

I cannot say strongly enough that over the years,
many people passed through my life and
those who fell away from God,
others who turned against Him,
ones who became religiously deluded, and worse,
several who went to outright evil,
were without exception people who did not forgive
one or both parents.

Proverbs has a sobering description of such people:
arrogant and vicious, never satisfied or grateful
and above all, spiritually blind.

Proverbs 30:11-15, 17 HCSB
There is a generation that curses its father
and does not bless its mother.
There is a generation that is pure in its own eyes,
yet is not washed from its filth.
There is a generation—how haughty its eyes
and pretentious its looks.
There is a generation whose teeth are swords,
whose fangs are knives,
devouring the oppressed from the land
and the needy from among mankind.

The leech has two daughters: "Give, Give!"
Three things are never satisfied;
four never say, "Enough!":
As for the eye that ridicules a father
and despises obedience to a mother,
may ravens of the valley pluck it out
and young vultures eat it.

There are also those who hate parents, loathe God,
and then become religious leaders . . .
for the motive of killing God on His servants.

After all, it was the religious who insisted and prevailed
that Jesus be crucified.

Should you find yourself in this list
and are justly stricken,
remember Jesus paid it all.

Our sins of hate and failure are already forgiven,
gone and buried.

So simple to solve!
Admit all to God and forsake
your old bitterness with parents.
Forgive them now and receive your own forgiveness.
Your 'criminal record' is expunged
and you have a verdict of 'not guilty!'

Oh, and don't forget . . . forgive YOU.

You can begin to change your heart, mind and spirit by
the simple exercise of gratitude.

Romans 1:18-32 reveals the consequences for the failure
to thank God. Verses 28-32 describe the moral downfall
of those who are ungrateful and 'disobedient to parents.'
The results range from foolishness to a depraved mind,
until they're finally 'filled with all unrighteousness.'
The end of the chapter, verse 32, states that the ungrateful
who become immoral are worthy of death!

God has a plan and purpose that has eternal meaning
for all your childhood and every suffering.
There is a purpose for you,
and your story is part of
His great Master Plan for Jesus Christ!

**Most of society's ills are not only the sins of the parents
but the unforgiveness of the sons and daughters.**

Why and How

WHY DO WE FORGIVE?

Forgiveness is God's heart in the Cross.
Being forgiven is the reason for the Cross.

He who died for all,
        did so to give the free gift of forgiveness—
            to mankind!

What He gave you freely, you cannot withhold from
others. Or you will lose your own freedom from sin's
punishment.

> *For if you forgive people their trespasses*
> *[their reckless and willful sins, leaving them,*
> *letting them go, and giving up resentment],*
> *your heavenly Father will also forgive you.*
>
> *But if you do not forgive others their trespasses*
> *[their reckless and willful sins, leaving them,*
> *letting them go, and giving up resentment],*
> *neither will your Father forgive you your trespasses.*
> *Matthew 6:14-15 AMPC*

The Cross of His Son's suffering is unimaginable and
so God gives you the perfect incentive: WHY to forgive.
You forgive to be forgiven!

Only then will you enjoy the peace with God that is your
own forgiveness.

You forfeit entirely your own forgiveness
    if you fail to forgive just one offence.

We want justice for the offender and mercy for ourselves.
But the Bible is clear, no one could mistake the meaning
of Jesus' words to the disciples.

    Only disciples – who have given all – will do
        the dreadful work of forgiving.

To forgive, you will die,
die to your rights and feelings.

    **But to fail to forgive is to die to God
    and your own destiny.**

HOW DO WE FORGIVE?

Forgiveness is Christ.
Forgiving others is virtually impossible.

So HOW indeed?

    *Come to Me,
    all who are weary and heavy-laden,
    and I will give you rest.
    Matthew 11:28 NASB*

    Jesus says only this: *"Come to Me."*

I was in anguish over someone I have worked with
for many years, always calling her to forgive a very
selfish mother. She would not. As a result, her blindness
remained, especially toward those she was abusing.

My burden for her soul was heavy,
    the effects of her life were exhausting.
    I was angry and weary, ready to give up.

I turned to the Lord and I sensed this sweet calling,
    full of compassion *for me!* "Come."

So I bowed to Him with all my burdened heart.
I could feel the grace of the Lord pour on me,
the extraordinary kindness of Christ,
and I knew He was taking the burden
    and giving me . . . Himself:
        His view, His counsel, His power.

I could sense His patient manner, His serene way of
dealing with us hysterical sheep, and I understood I was
to stay with her – as long as it took – until she came to
repentance and forgiveness.

The marvelous grace of Christ gave me the power to
forgive her completely for tons of wrongs. And the Lord's
sweet love caused me to yearn to see her the next day.

I discovered that almost overnight this woman, dear to
God, had completely repented, fully forgiven, and most
amazingly, assumed responsibility for her failure to
accept her life as a gift from God. No longer was it the
parent's evil, she knew that her only problem was her
response of rebellion to her mother.

She was filled with wisdom and light. I merely listened and marveled at the power of forgiveness.

God had done it all. We wept together and we were drenched in the love of Christ for each other and for Him!

I have a favorite verse . . . tried and true.

> *Let be and be still, and know*
> *(recognize and understand) that I am God.*
> *Psalm 46:10 AMPC*

Let be.

Let the situation BE what it is and LET God handle it.
Bow to the Lord, open your hands,
lift them to God and say,
    "I accept the situation. You are God!"

Be Still.

Offenses and hurts tempt us to believe that God is not good enough to defend and not powerful enough to change the situation. Your faith is under attack.

Let BE and Be still. Listen, be quiet, don't talk, and you will soon know that . . .

God is God.

You can grip a situation or a wrong so tightly that
    you quench the Spirit's move.
You can worry yourself into a tizzy and
    you have taken over God's chair to rule,
    even if only in thought and anguish.

Until you *'release it, leave it, let it drop,'* God will not move.

He waits for you to LET Him be God.
Stop trying to fix it.
Give up control, anguishing thoughts,
imagined solutions.

**Letting go is a skill to learn
and a strength to acquire.**

*And whenever you stand praying,
if you have anything against anyone,
forgive him and let it drop (leave it, let it go),
in order that your Father Who is in heaven may
also forgive you your [own] failings
and shortcomings and let them drop.*

*But if you do not forgive, neither will your Father in heaven
forgive your failings and shortcomings.*
Mark 11:25-26 AMPC

Jesus puts the 'how' in simple terms:

*forgive him, let it drop (leave it, let it go),
leaving (the sins), letting them go,
and giving up resentment]* . . .

And that is very hard work because to forgive is to die a
little, or more often a lot.

To forgive, you will die to your rights and feelings.
But to fail to forgive is to die to God
and your own destiny.

RELEASE YOUR GRIEF TO JESUS

I read this verse and I was amazed.
No one ever told me that Jesus took on our griefs and
sorrows! I thought He only took away our sins.
Jesus bore my sins but also the sins *against* me.

> *Surely our griefs He Himself bore,*
> *And our sorrows He carried.*
> Isaiah 53:4 NASB

I saw that amazingly, He bore my griefs of sin, regret,
disappointment, and suffering at the hands of others! So
I asked Him also to carry away my sorrows of injustice,
lies and betrayals.

I gave it all to Jesus and asked Him to take what I couldn't
release. It was as if He was saying:
"I bore it all Myself! You don't have to carry it."

Many times Christ has taken out of my soul and heart,
even out of my memory, those terrible griefs and painful
sorrows.
I have offered my pains to the Cross
where Jesus took them all.
A deep relief and freedom are His gift back to you.

I have taught others to release to Christ all their pain of
sufferings.

Get on your knees and submit to Him.
Lift your open hands to Him and declare that
you release your 'griefs and sorrows' to Him.

We are but sheep and sheep cannot bear burdens.
We humans cannot bear the burden of normal life,
much less the suffering that is inevitable for
"all who desire to live godly in Christ Jesus
will be persecuted" (2 Timothy 3:12 NASB).

Having raised sheep I know well that sheep can't be
disturbed or frightened. They can't bear suffering or fear.
They need 'still waters.'

We are Jesus' sheep and He is the good shepherd.
Let Him have all your problems,
wrongs, and sufferings.
He will carry it all for you,
instead of you.

CHRIST, THE FORGIVER

Forgiveness is necessary, critical, lifesaving . . .
but in your worst situations, utterly impossible.

When you set yourself on a course of serious forgiveness,
you will discover Him who IS forgiveness,
Who gave forgiveness.

You meet the Source of forgiveness living within you, and
forgiveness and grace flow without hindrance toward
others, so long as you bow to this One Who forgives YOU
in a constant unbroken river of grace.

Faith and Mountains

When searching the Word to learn forgiveness, Mark 11 was the first passage of my study.

Jesus had cursed a fig tree that didn't yield fruit for Him, even though it was not the season for figs. And the next day, that very bush was dead from the roots up. The disciples saw it and were astonished . . .

> *And Jesus answered them, "Have faith in God.*
> *Truly, I say to you, whoever says to this mountain,*
> *'Be taken up and thrown into the sea',*
> *and does not doubt in his heart, but believes*
> *that what he says will come to pass,*
> *it will be done for him.*
> *Therefore I tell you, whatever you ask in prayer,*
> *believe that you have received it, and it will be yours."*
> *Mark 11:22-24 ESV*

I was familiar with this scripture. I had always wanted this level of faith, to speak and see obstacles removed.

I once was among many enthusiastic believers who wanted to be movers of big mountains. This was the promise of Jesus Himself to His twelve disciples. I saw believers taking hold of this, speaking to whatever mountain obstacle they had and commanding it into the sea.

I had spoken to mountains also, but I was never certain the mountain even budged.

I continued reading and it seemed I had never seen this verse before!

> *Whenever you stand praying,*
> *if you have anything against anyone,*
> *forgive him [drop the issue, let it go], so that*
> *your Father who is in heaven will also forgive you*
> *your transgressions and wrongdoings*
> *[against Him and others].*
> *["But if you do not forgive, neither will*
> *your Father in heaven forgive your transgressions."]*
> *Mark 11:25-26 AMP (emphasis mine)*

I was shocked to understand that Jesus gave a condition to mountain-moving prayer. The condition to faith for such power was *forgiveness*.

Forgiveness yields faith in God's power
    and unforgiveness is the obstacle to faith
        in God Himself.

I realized that unforgiveness was itself a mountain.
    Of course! If we don't forgive, it is unbelief
    in what God has done.
        And our faith in God's power
        and His hearing us is destroyed.

God does not hear the prayer of one who refuses to forgive! By vague guilt and a sense of disconnect, we know that He is not available to us and our prayers are not answered. And we wonder why!

In contrast, God does hear the prayer of the forgiver and grants faith equal to a mountain of trouble.

Power with God comes from forgiving anyone with whom we have an offense, and having received forgiveness for our wrongs *"against Him and others."*

I vividly experienced this very thing the day before I was to write this chapter.

IN THE FEAR OF GOD

The presence of the Holy Spirit came on me powerfully and suddenly. I began to weep and tell the Lord, "I cannot write this book. I am unworthy for such a holy subject. I can't do it!"

I wept and wept, still telling Him I was totally unworthy. And then a great fear of God came upon me. I shook and wept. This went on for at least an hour and I could only fall on my knees and cry, "Oh God!" I came to peace finally, but I asked Him to show me what had happened to elicit such fear of Him.

The next morning as I woke up, I knew. A person I had known for years, and loved, became religious, superior, and very disloyal. This one was often inflicting pain on people I love and on me also.

We didn't have close contact, so I wasn't as much aware of their cruelty. But something had happened to remind me of their religious wickedness, and I had not stopped to deal with my heart's response.

Altogether Forgiven

That morning I realized I had never fully forgiven this person. I had not completely 'let it go' and released the offenses *from my heart*. I quickly dealt with that and confessed my own sin. I asked the Lord to give me His love and show me how to pray for my enemy. Now when the Lord gives His word, I will be able to speak His will to the mountain of Satan's domain over this person and the stronghold will jump into the sea.

Forgiveness has a mighty power to make everyone free!
        The offender and the offended.
        Every person and every thing was created
        to produce fruit for Jesus, Son of God.

I have seen many mountains cast into the sea. The sea, the place where demon-filled pigs were sent. The Word of God's power will move mountains of sin and rebellion into the sea, to set people free of guilt and oppression.

This promise is real and practical. The power is available. It depends only on the obedience to forgive *"anything against anyone."*

We can all have a monumental ministry called
        Moving Mountains by Forgiveness.

   **And people are set free
        to live and bear fruit for Jesus!**

In this situation, I was fully reconciled to God by His mercy. But I can tell you that I am more sober about forgiveness than ever.

Forgiveness cannot be partial, saving some part of the offense and not letting it go. I see clearly that if I fail to forgive just one person, I have lost entirely my own forgiveness. I would stand before my God with all the sin of my entire life still on me. I would have forfeited my eternal inheritance and any reward for years of obedience. It all would vanish, and all that would be left is me with all my sin.

Never have I seen with such clarity that forgiveness is life and death, an eternal matter.

I would be in heaven, as one born again, but a complete failure and separated from the presence of Christ. And that would be eternally unbearable!

Work at living in peace with everyone,
and work at living a holy life,
for those who are not holy will not see the Lord.
Hebrews 12:14 NLT

Through forgiveness you can be at peace with one who is not at peace with you!

"Is God that hard?"

God is that just! He is so jealous that His Beloved Son shall not have suffered in vain. To reject His gift of forgiveness is to reject God Himself and to trample underfoot the blood of Jesus.

This is why I ask fervently to know the Cross of Jesus. I want to receive all He has given and, in the fear of God, I want Christ to have the glory He deserves from all He suffered!

As long as there is a breath of life, there will be
      ever new offenses to forgive and
      fresh mistakes for which we need to be forgiven.

No matter our faithfulness to God, unforgiveness can
defeat us at any turn, and to such a degree that we incur
the wrath of God, same as any unrepentant sinner.

      Life is the great ongoing test of our love for God
      and the exposure of our love of self.

Your Worst Enemy

You have an enemy of your destiny. In fact, this is your worst enemy, one who is totally against you, often corrupts you, and gets you constantly into trouble.

This enemy fails you, hates God, and cares only about itself. It compels you to do what you don't want to do, and drags you where you wish you hadn't gone.

It is the most dangerous of all your enemies and the hardest to forgive.

**Look in the mirror
and you will see your worst enemy.**

Have you ever tried to forgive YOU? Oh, you have so many offenses with what you have done!
That forgiveness is a mountain hidden in your soul.

In fact, this is usually that last person you will think of
as an enemy to forgive.

We have done what can't be undone
and the regret is life long.

*For what I am doing, I do not understand;
for I am not practicing what I would like to do,
but I am doing the very thing I hate.*

*So now, no longer am I the one doing it,
but sin which dwells in me.*

> *For I know that nothing good dwells in me,*
> *that is, in my flesh; for the willing is present in me,*
> *but the doing of the good is not.*
> *Romans 7:15, 17-18 NASB*

Paul experienced this and cried out in his helplessness. He had an alive conscience that knew God's law and ways, but he had no power to stop failing, and no solution.

This is the inevitable experience of a true believer.
> We come to the futility of our efforts,
> the failure of our character,
> and it is excruciating.

The man was in that terrible struggle within, the flesh warring against the spirit. Paul's answer and liberty was Christ.

> *Therefore there is now no condemnation*
> *for **those who are in Christ Jesus**.*
> *For the law of the spirit of life in Christ Jesus*
> *has set you free from the law of sin and of death.*
> *Romans 8:1-2 NASB (emphasis mine)*

The truth we learn is that we died with Christ,
> and our new life was resurrected with Him.

Or are you unaware that
all of us who were baptized into Christ Jesus
were baptized into His death?
Therefore, we were buried with Him by baptism into death,
in order that, just as Christ was raised from the dead
by the glory of the Father,
so we too may walk in a new way of life.
Romans 6:3-4 HCSB

There is overwhelming grace when you forgive yourself. For some, this is the last forgiveness and perhaps the most powerful to give you freedom from guilt and self-hatred.

FALSE GUILT

When I was young in the Lord, I had a tendency to assume the wrong things were my fault. Someone would wrong me greatly and I'd think his behavior was my fault. "Somehow I must have evoked it."

I was consumed in guilt and though I confessed 'my' sin, I had no sweet sense of peace from Jesus' forgiveness. I was much in prayer about it and the Lord said clearly,
"I did not pay for what you did not do.
There is no blood sacrifice
when you are innocent."

And my eyes were opened to a great liberty. It became so clear that the other party was completely responsible, not me. I cannot be forgiven for what I did not do! My peace came only when I gave up my false guilt and recognized the true guilt of the offender.

People blame.

Even believers dump their guilt wherever they can.
Blame is inherent in humanity, from the Garden.
    The man blamed the woman,
        the woman blamed the serpent.

All forgiveness requires God's help to sort out real guilt
and false guilt. And it is a joyful and blessed assignment,
because no matter the human mess, you can experience
the cleansing of your heart before God.

The Spirit shares God's reality, and either way, you
forgive or you are forgiven.

> *For You, Lord, are good and ready to forgive,*
> *And abundant in lovingkindness to all*
> *who call upon You.*
> Psalm 86:5 NASB

> *If You, Lord, should mark iniquities, O Lord, who could stand?*
> *But there is forgiveness with You,*
> *That You may be feared.*
> Psalm 130:3-4 NASB

Offended With God

John the Baptist was in prison, knowing his fate at the hands of Herod. He was soon to be beheaded for obeying God and confronting Herod.

But Jesus didn't come to set him free,
       and John was left offended with the Lord.

Doubts in Christ would be easy in such a crisis.
John sent to Jesus to ask:

> *"Are you the Expected One*
> *or do we look for someone else?"*
> *Matthew 11:3 NASB*

"You leave me here to die!
       Are You really who You claim to be?"

Jesus was doing many miracles at the time and He pointed to them as proof in His answer.
       Then He continued:

> *"And blessed [joyful, spiritually favored by God]*
> *is he who does not take offense at Me."*
> *Luke 7:23 AMP*

It's important to know that when cruel injustice comes to us and we aren't rescued out of it, we can be offended with Christ who could have saved us and . . . didn't!

I have been hurt with the Lord many times because He didn't remove me, even from danger! And this scripture in Luke is the answer the Holy Spirit would give me.

I have prayed, "Lord, I want that blessing – the joy and favor of God – that belongs to those who are not offended with YOU for what You allow me to suffer from the abuse of others!"

When we are disappointed in God's action and inaction, we must let go of our offenses with Him.

> *And blessed[1]*
> *(happy – with life-joy and satisfaction in God's favor and*
> *salvation, apart from outward conditions – and to be envied)*
> *is he who takes no offense in Me and who is not*
> *hurt or resentful or annoyed or repelled or made to stumble*
> *[whatever may occur].*
> *Luke 7:23 AMPC*

I have experienced this, so I believe God gives His presence and grace in situations where He seems to be indifferent to our plight. I am confident that Jesus' word and the grace of God were sufficient for John to make peace with God before he died.

God is faithful and His ways are always vindicated!

Every crisis has a divine purpose, unseen and unimaginable. In the middle of the disaster, we bow to Him Who IS God and cling to His goodness, trusting in His ways.

For our momentary, light distress [this passing trouble]
*is producing for us an **eternal weight of glory [a fullness]***
beyond all measure [surpassing all comparisons,
a transcendent splendor and an endless blessedness]!

So we look not at the things which are seen,
but at the things which are unseen;
for the things which are visible are temporal
*[just brief and fleeting], but **the things which***
are invisible are everlasting and imperishable.
2 Corinthians 4:17-18 AMP (emphasis mine)

The verse above was given to me during my brief cancer
episode. It seemed unimaginable, but still I clung to it and
repeated it until it was rooted in my heart.

. . . in a humble (gentle, modest) spirit receive and welcome
the Word which [implanted and rooted in your hearts]
contains the power to save your souls.
James 1:21b AMPC

I don't know all of God's glorious purpose for His Son,
but I can say I am more blessed today than ever . . .
blessed with the presence and purpose of God,
ever unfolding and amazing.

When forgiveness is your constant, you will come to find
yourself inside a faith that knows God's forgiveness for all
mankind.

You will be hard to offend and you will be able, by the indwelling power of Christ, to *"resist not the evil men do to you."* This hardest of all commands is actually performed by Christ Himself, Who alone can obey such an immovable way of Life.

In His union with the Father,
Jesus knew all things were in His Sovereign Hands.
    So He was ever above and beyond
    the fray of man and devils.

---

[1] The word *blessed* in Greek (Strong's #3107): "Being blessed is equivalent to having God's kingdom within one's heart."

Have You Forgiven God?

Early in my walk with the Lord, I stayed in an Episcopal Convent. There I met God in the incredible healing of my mother's death that occurred when I was 14.

My reconciliation with God was in hearing this:
> "Yes, I took your mother, just as you suspected.
> I hold the keys to hell and to death."

After I absorbed that shocking truth,
He continued with the strangest word of all:
> "Now forgive Me."

I couldn't take that in. How do you forgive GOD?

Though I cannot now recall its title, I had a book in my suitcase by Dr. Paul Tournier. I opened it at random and my eyes fell instantly on the following statement:

> "We all have offenses with God
> for which we need to forgive Him."

In that moment I had God's grace to simply agree,
> "Yes, I forgive you, Lord."

I walked out of that convent with an enormous sense of having been cleansed and made whole. God had come to find me.

He had condescended to make peace with me,
  when the offense was in me!
    I was sure I had become a new person and
      life proved it to be true.

Yet I was to revisit that confrontation again and again.

   "Lord, I sense I have unforgiveness.
    Who have I not forgiven?"
      "You have not forgiven Me."

At last I went to Him about it. "Ok, let's deal with this, Lord. How can one have the audacity to forgive You, Who are never wrong and never wrong anyone?" I clearly heard, "Look it up in the dictionary."

The dictionary definition solved it.

  "Forgiveness is releasing a person who has hurt you."

At last I understood. God had hurt me, but He had not wronged me. That was the difference.

By allowing circumstances, sending crosses to me,
  He had definitely hurt me . . .
  but never, ever did He wrong me!

The Bible is so clear as to be shocking on this subject: God is God.

He is in absolute, unquestionable control of everything. What comes to me must pass through His hand first. Witness Job.

Witness Peter: *"Satan has demanded permission to sift you like wheat; but I have prayed for you (Luke 22:31-32 NASB)."*

Apparently, Satan must ask permission to touch God's servants. Whatever comes, comes from God.
Whatever is allowed, is allowed by Him.

We like Romans 8:28 (NKJV) –

> *All things work together for good to those who love God, to those who are the called according to His purpose.*

Now there is a statement of absolute sovereignty . . . but it is exclusive. It doesn't apply to everyone, that is clear.

God's sovereignty abides over those who love Him
and who are walking in obedience to His calling,
which is the final exaltation of Christ!

All things will serve God's purpose in the end.

He rules over circumstance and history. Yet you are utterly free to choose. He will let you decide to reject Him and disobey Him. But then you will also live with HIS choice of the consequences.

Altogether Forgiven

Always I can come back under the sovereign shield of God's loving will. But when I leave His ruling throne and strike out on my own way,
destruction and chaos are *my* choice.

God is not to blame.

We fallen race of humans were born with a primal suspicion of God and an inherent drive to supplant Him. To forgive Him is to accept His choices and chastening by believing and having seen that He is good and loving.

We must come to know
that truly **He is God and there is no other—**
not Satan, not man, and especially not me.

You are my servant.
You have been chosen to know me, believe in me,
and understand that I alone am God.
There is no other God –
there never has been and there never will be.
Isaiah 43:10 NLT

SEE ALSO: Deuteronomy 4:35, 39; 1 Kings 8:60; Isaiah 44:8;
45:5, 14, 21-22; 46:9; Joel 2:27

A Matter of the Heart

Forgiveness is a work, yes. But it is not a work in the sheer grit of determination to forgive. To forgive is this alone: Seeking God until you come to intimate fellowship with His heart about the issue and the person.

Someone asked me with real sincerity,
      "How do I know if I have forgiven?"
My answer was brief.
      "When you love your enemy."

Forgiveness is a choice, yes. But after the will to forgive, it is not a mental matter. As the scriptures make clear, forgive . . . "from your heart."

When you are hurt, the pain goes to your heart first,
      then your mind.

      A broken heart is a heart wounded and wronged.
      Its healing comes only through God's loving grace
      and His own forgiveness of your persecutor.

Offenses are gifts that thrust you into God's presence by sheer need of survival.

In fellowship with Him,
      He gives the resolution in His will,
      the forgiveness you need . . .
            and that most impossible thing:
            Love for your enemy.

For forgiveness to be genuine and complete,
the forgiving must reach down and issue from the heart.

LOVE YOUR ENEMY

Jesus said to His disciples:

> *"You have heard that it was said,*
> *'YOU SHALL LOVE YOUR NEIGHBOR*
> *AND HATE YOUR ENEMY.'*
> *But I say to you, love your enemies and*
> *pray for those who persecute you,*
> *so that you may be sons of your Father who is in heaven;*
> *for He causes His sun to rise on the evil and the good,*
> *and sends rain on the righteous and the unrighteous.*
> *For if you love those who love you,*
> *what reward do you have?*
> *Do not even the tax collectors do the same?"*
> Matthew 5:43-48 NASB

Love is not sentiment nor is it feelings.

At one time I begged the Lord for love for an ongoing
enemy. The love *I* wanted never came.
I never had feelings of warm love for her.
That alone was the measure of love,
or so I thought.

But when I sought the Lord about it, He said,
"You are praying for the salvation of her soul."

I sensed that no one else in the world was praying for her as fervently as I was.

He assured me that *this was genuine love.* I understood that in God's view,

Love is commitment, not feelings.

Love is not real love until you care about the eternal soul of your enemy and cry out for God's healing for them. Feelings are irrelevant.

When you get in harmony with God about your enemy, His desires become your desires, and His love compels you to join His heart of Love above all.

On the other hand, God might very well release you of further responsibility for rebellious persons. The disciples were told to wipe the dust off their feet when leaving a town that refused to hear them. It meant they had no further duty toward the souls there.

That too, is God's love for you, the victim. He sets you free of any further responsibility. Your separation from the enemy is the end of the matter.

THE REAL TREASURE

God has a purpose above all else.

His aim in all human events, all suffering,
and all heartache is this:
    That we come to know, with the deepest intimacy,
        God and the Son whom He has sent.

Now this is eternal life:
that they may know You, the only true
[supreme and sovereign] God and
[in the same manner] know
Jesus [as the] Christ whom You have sent.
John 17:3 AMP

The only riches on earth are found in coming to
'understand and know' God.

Job's awful suffering had its culmination in 'seeing God.'
Until then Job knew God only by 'the hearing of the ear.'
And his life was changed from one of misery
to one of healing for his enemies,
who had been his friends of torment.

Thus says the LORD,
"Let not a wise man boast of his wisdom,
and let not the mighty man boast of his might,
let not a rich man boast of his riches;
but let him who boasts boast of this,
that he understands and knows Me,
that I am the LORD WHO EXERCISES LOVINGKINDNESS,
justice and righteousness on earth;
for I delight in these things," declares the LORD.
JEREMIAH 9:23-24 NASB

The Biblical Map of Forgiveness

Jesus gently leads us lambs
to the School of Forgiveness,
down the road marked "Real Life."

The Little Child Forgives

A deep and crucial lesson was taught by our Lord in Matthew 18. A lesson which began with a question of Jesus by the ambitious disciples:

"Who is the greatest in the kingdom of heaven?"

It was an honest inquiry, born of human tendency, and Jesus answered it with loving respect, completely and fully in this chapter. But His answer did not fit their ambitious question.

Jesus called a little child to Himself and put him in the midst of them. This small, living illustration of His answer was provided so that by the visual, they could comprehend the reality of what He was about to teach. And the object of the lesson would be . . .

all aspects of forgiveness.

I assure you and most solemnly say to you, unless you repent [that is, change your inner self—your old way of thinking, live changed lives] and become like children [trusting, humble, and forgiving], you will never enter the kingdom of heaven.

Therefore, whoever humbles himself like this child is greatest in the kingdom of heaven.
Matthew 18:3-4 AMP

A startling answer! Certainly not the one they expected.

Mankind ever believes that power and ability are the peaks of achievement, of importance, and worth.

God's values are just the opposite and that is our crisis with Him.

Humanity believes in "up."
Jesus ever calls us to go "down."

The word "change" in this scripture doesn't mean become something bigger. It means change into what you *should* be.

The Greek meaning is "turn around and go back."
Become what you *used to be* . . . a child.

The inference is that
you have gone the wrong way and gotten lost.
You must go back to where you were long ago.

A CHILD FORGIVES

Jesus describes a little child as
"[trusting, lowly, loving, forgiving] (AMPC)."

A little child is without the guile of the adult.

A little child truly is trusting, lowly, loving, and forgiving. Mistreat a child and ask forgiveness. They will hug and kiss you with lavish forgiveness, delighted to give it. Here is the picture of what we are to be!

Then Jesus links Himself to the child and the child to Him. Christ is with the child in us. He puts His stake with the 'little' child as *"greatest in the kingdom."*

> *And whoever receives and accepts and welcomes one*
> *little child like this for My sake and in My name*
> *receives and accepts and welcomes Me.*
> Matthew 18:5 AMP

The child He refers to is not only the child in their midst, not the children of their world, but also the child within, buried in those adults who stood before Him.

The child is the primal and vulnerable being
who yet lives in every adult—
> the real self, the unsophisticated, dependent being
> with no pretense and no sufficiency.

Jesus said not just child but "little child."

Early on as children, we learn to deceive, to pretend. Very young we take on the lies of life: self-sufficiency, self-indulgence, and above all, self-protection.

Adultness, which is to say . . . pride.

The awful truth about us at our raw core is that we will ever be – from this Perilous Now through the Unknown Future, even into the Eternal Forever – only a child.

> Needy and utterly incapable, therefore . . .
> desperately dependent.

Another way to say "poor in spirit"? A beggar.
This is the humility of the child,
and! the frightening human crisis—
     having no value by virtue of being nothing,
     in total inability.
          But the child has infinite worth
          beyond counting to our Father.

God is, above all, a Father who longs for His children
          to be real children who need a Father.

Jesus is "joined" only to the inner child in us,
     that vulnerable and honest being,
          void of these adult attributes:
               masks and pretense,
               effort and strife,
               lying and trying.

Jesus introduced the subject, and then He gave several
illustrations. The key – the core of the discourse – is the
open reality of the child.

A 'little' child lives in utter dependence and that is what
God wants.

**Poverty possesses the kingdom of a heavenly life
even in earth's hostile ground.**

LITTLE ONES WHO STUMBLE

The first and deepest wounds of the soul
are the wrongs of family and authorities inflicted on
the helpless child.

Those primal hurts are buried at the bottom of the well of our soul's story. Few there are who dig out the hurts, tell the story to their heart, and with God . . . forgive.

When leaders/parents cause children to stumble, the Father is horrified. Jesus exposed that horror in Matthew 18, showing that His compassion is with the "little ones."

But whoever causes one of these little ones who believe in Me
to stumble, it would be better for him to have
a heavy millstone hung around his neck,
and to be drowned in the depth of the sea.
Matthew 18:6 NASB

Better to be dead than cause a child to learn sin!

As we learned in "Faith and Mountains," the 'depth of the sea' stands for the place of sin's deposit, the home of demons, where God buries the rebellious. The sea stands for the great abode of His rejection, symbol of endless separation from God.

Parents,
any who assume the role of parent in cruel dictatorship,
despots and dominators who never admit their iniquity,
those who tyrannize the vulnerable child within us—
ALL will live flailing in a perpetual drowning,
weighted with a millstone of guilt
under God's Parental Eye.

Better to be dead!

Woe to the world for such
temptations to sin and influences to do wrong!
Matthew 18:7 AMPC

Woe means grief . . .
The very world of both parent and child suffers and
heaves under the sins not confessed and so not forgiven.
And the sins are inherited and perpetuated, on and on.

Generation to generation,
until the world is filled with woe.

All people in the range of such offenses suffer in the
aftermath of the sins of leaders-and-parents and the
hurts of "children." All the world pays. And all the world
grieves.

Woe and grief – to the world.
Woe and grief also
to the person who makes a little one stumble.

It is necessary that temptations come,
but woe to the person on whose account
or by whom the temptation comes!
Matthew 18:7 AMPC

Jesus is always real. Adam's offspring are wicked
monsters. All of us! Pains and hurt to the "little one" are
inevitable, a terrible tragedy and the experience of us all.

We grown-up children are all wounded in some way,
and we go into some deep hiding place of the soul,
a place of the loss-of-self by unbalmed pain.

And so the Shepherd searches through the unlit labyrinth
of the soul . . . for the lost lamb. But few, so few, will let
themselves be "found" and
  their wounds closed by the cure of forgiving.

MY HAND, MY EYE

From utter sympathy for little ones abused, suddenly,
  abruptly Jesus changed the focus.

*If your hand or your foot causes you to sin
    cut it off and throw it away.
It is better for you to enter life maimed or crippled than to
have two hands or two feet and be thrown into eternal fire.*

*And if your eye causes you to sin,
    gouge it out and throw it away.
It is better for you to enter life with one eye than to
have two eyes and be thrown into the fire of hell.
Matthew 18:8-9 NIV*

The problem, still being unfolded, turns against "me" –
    my precious hand,
      my very foot, and even . . .
        my own eye.

Such drastic measures, spoken of as a violence to oneself!
A self-surgery of the sick-sin you have contracted
by exposure, but of which you will have become the
infectious carrier.

    Drastic measures, stripping solution.
      A picture of shocking self-annihilation.

"I, the abused, am told to hurt myself?"
Yes, my problem is . . . *me*.

My own doing, choosing, seeing.

The problem is not what was inflicted on me.
The problem is three "what's":

> What I *did* because of it;
> What I *chose to be* in reaction to it;
> What I *see and believe* by the influence of it.

The problem is me, my and mine.
Not them or theirs, his or hers.
Mine alone.

Another's abuse of me becomes a crisis of my response,
not a nightmare of their mistreatment.

True repentance is assuming all responsibility for
> who you are and have become.
> There is one problem only in life's cruelty:
> > my response to it.

Hand is doing.
> I will want to do what has been done to me.

Foot is choosing.
> My step goes in the direction of my bitterness.

Eye is the lens through which I perceive things.
> My chosen view is clouded and distorted
> by the imprint of my suffering.

My anguish and anger is not about what is *done to me!*
It is *what I become* by my deep-rooted response to wrongs.

A Bible teacher once said to me, "No one knows what
I have suffered." I replied, "I could also say that, but I
discovered that most of my suffering was the pain of
wounded pride."

LOST LAMBS

The terrors of the "child" cannot be faced.
The powerlessness of the "child" cannot be endured. Our
Eminent Adult must rise up,
> the noble liar who pushes through and "does it,"
> and then the simplicity of the child is gone.
> > The spontaneity of the child is lost.
So Jesus says, "Repent," which means 'turn around.'

Your inner child holds the original secret of your identity.
Only the childlike have the capacity for primal joy in life.

> And . . . most important,
> **the child alone forgives.**

Most of us adults have lost the child within, the essential
created being, our "little" self.

The Shepherd wants His real lambs, and He moves
to recover those captured in the bramble of pain . . .
pleading but not knowing if they're heard.

That lamb is you. And me. And the Shepherd does hear.

If any man has a hundred sheep,
and one of them has gone astray,
does he not leave the ninety-nine on the mountains
and go and search for the one that is straying?

And if it turns out that he finds it, truly I say to you,
he rejoices over it more than the ninety-nine
which have not gone astray.

So it is not the will of your Father who is in heaven
that one of these little ones perish.
Matthew 18:12-14 NASB

By His gentle stream in your life, He will move your child out of its driven hiding place, stand 'you' in the midst of your life, and say, "To this one *alone* belongs the Kingdom."

God brings us – sometimes by force – to the humility of that little self.

I have wandered away like a lost sheep; come and find me,
for I have not forgotten Your commands.
Psalm 119:176 NLT

This priceless lesson of Jesus, complete in Matthew 18, has its sections and its culmination. In the end, the subject is exposed: forgiveness. But to get there Jesus builds a slow pathway.
Forgiveness – being so critical an issue –
calls for a patient pursuit.

In His gracious fashion, Jesus moves toward His intent with the patience of a Shepherd, unhurried, waiting to see that these sheep drink the lessons and follow along behind Him.

Forgiveness is a deep well
that opens a flowing fountain of peace with God.

Each person must dig out with patience and prayer,
 the dirty malice of his secret heart,
 until he is washed with the liberating Holy Blood.

BECOMING A CHILD

The Kingdom is given to the child. The Kingdom is a
home only for the child.

But know this, you who want to repent and go back
to the simplicity of a child.
 You cannot find your lost lamb.
 Only the Shepherd can.
You dare not create a fake childlikeness or you will be
merely childish.

When you are willing . . .
 the Holy Spirit takes charge
 to bring you down to a child before God.

And His work will be to *decrease you, detach you, and
increase Christ in you.* Christ Himself will live His holy
childhood in you.

Make childlikeness your surrender and prayer,
 but not your project.

To be a child is an inward change,
> produced by the Spirit's application of the cross.
> It is not an outward behavior.

Our adult independence! *That* must be slain.

Like Father, Like Son

Jesus lived as a leaning child.
Stop and notice His reliance on His Father and His joy to be there!

Most assuredly I say to you,
the Son can do nothing of Himself,
but what He sees the Father do;
for whatever He does, the Son also does in like manner.
John 5:19 NKJV

Jesus lived as a Child unto God.
Utterly dependent, ever vulnerable to His will.

We never note that Jesus lived as a Child, in the barren reality of human weakness.

We note His power, His dominion.
We see Jesus as the ultimate powerful person.

He was God, but He came to earth as a common human
Who never needed to be in charge.

On this earth, everything Jesus had and all He was
came from the Father,
under whose wings He settled . . . as a Child.

He walked and lived as a Son,
receiving all things from His Heavenly Father:
His power, His direction,
His very thoughts.
All were derived.

I can of Myself do nothing.
As I hear, I judge; and My judgment is righteous
because I do not seek My own will but the will of the Father
who sent me.
John 5:30 NKJV

Jesus ever gave His identity as the Son of God. Or the Son of Man. He was of Another, as a child is. He was a son! He needed no personal title for His ego. He was His Father's child, He required no individuality, needed no self-supporting hallmark of His own making. Jesus was content to live solely by the specialness of Another – His dear Father.

Because of this willingness to be swallowed into the Father as a subordinate Child, He manifested the awesome authority of Very God, as a trusted representative and not a master.

The authority of the kingdom is available only to "the little child."

Authority WITH God comes when I take my place as His dependent child. I can then make claims upon Him based on my position. I need no merit for my appeal.

Fear not, little flock, for it is your Father's
good pleasure to give you the kingdom.
Luke 12:32 ESV

I enjoy the rights of my birth, given and secured FOR me, not earned BY me.

I am God's child! In reality.

. . . who were born, not of blood, nor of the will of the flesh,
nor of the will of man, but **of God.**
John 1:13 NKJV

I must live in the vulnerability – even the helplessness –
that is my real state. That is what puts me into the place
of being childlike. Just reality.

Jesus was describing His own way of living,
and giving us the same way to enter the kingdom,
when He said,

> *Truly, I say to you, unless you turn*
> *and become like children,*
> *you will never enter the kingdom of heaven.*
> *Matthew 18:3 ESV*

Be what you are . . . for you are a child! Being a child puts
you in the position to receive a Father and all the rights of
His Position. Only as you are a child are you able to have
a Father.

Be an independent, self-sufficient adult and
you have lost the kingdom . . .
and your Dear Protective Father.

Position! The universe is all about position! Power is
about position.

Let God have His position, be in yours (as a child), and
power over life is natural. Authority FOR God flows from
our surrender to being His child, deriving everything
from Him, subject to His rule.

How Many Times?

*Then Peter came to Him and said, "Lord, how many times
could my brother sin against me and I forgive him?
As many as seven times?"
"I tell you, not as many as seven," Jesus said to him,
"but seventy times seven.
Matthew 18:21-22 HCSB*

I have always wondered if Peter's question was evoked by
Jesus' words from verse 6:

*"But whoever causes the downfall of
one of these little ones who believe in Me—
it would be better for him if a heavy millstone
were hung around his neck
and he were drowned in the depths of the sea!"
Matthew 18:6 HCSB*

Was Peter thinking of himself as one who had
experienced being made to stumble as a little child? His
question is certainly from one who has thought about the
issue of forgiveness.

Seven is the great number of spiritual perfection.
The Rabbis taught that you were only obligated to forgive
seven times. And Jesus took that limited number and
exploded it.

The Lord doesn't mean for us to forgive 490 times.
He means to forgive on and on and on.
And on.

I know a woman of God who was married to a cruel man.

Every day she purposed to give him a clean slate,
    remembering no sins of yesterday.
He had a fresh start each day –
    with no grudges, accusations, or bitter words.

This went on for some 25 years through much suffering.
She forgave him 9,125 times and more.
That is certainly more than 490!

      During those years, she remained blessed
        under God's grace.

At the end of her husband's life, this woman's prayers for his soul were answered, and he went to God having been set free of sin.

Confronting the Sinner

This rich chapter is a blueprint of the process of reconciliation, each phase leading into the next and building upon each level. From the search and recovery of the lost lamb – seeming to change the subject – Jesus then moves to the next matter.

If another believer sins against you,
go privately and point out the offense.
If the other person listens and confesses it,
you have won that person back.
Matthew 18:15 NLT

Essential in the process of forgiveness is the phase of confrontation.

God alone can help you name the wrong,
object to the injury, and stand up to the offender
by the clean energy of honest anguish.

Only Christ in you can manage this delicate matter. This is entirely about being humbly led of the Holy Spirit into the will of God. He wants us to be ministers of reconciliation.

Confrontation is a kindness.
Love is caring for another's eternal destiny and if not, then it is not love.

Confrontation is loving the offender enough to help them see their wrong. It is loving yourself enough to object.

If your brother sins, go and show him his fault in private;
if he listens and pays attention to you,
you have won back your brother.
Matthew 18:15 AMP

In the pain of a deep wrong, Jesus demands a spiritual integrity and godly responsibility. Tell *first* the one who did the wrong. And He added that it should be a private confrontation, with no one else present.

The brave 'child' wants to say, "Ouch, you hurt me!"
The cowardly 'adult' would rather gossip.

Confrontation is a nightmare, a dread,
and an agony sometimes worse than the offense.

To open yourself up is to welcome a possible attack,
to hazard rejection and abuse. It is risking your own
reputation and . . . the relationship involved.

Confrontation takes the courage of the 'child'
and is one vital step in the long journey
that is mutual forgiveness
and full reconciliation.

How easy it is to forgive one who will hear your pain and see his wrong! All is resolved if that one listens. And you have not smeared his reputation, slandered his name, and heaped upon yourself a fresh load of guilt by disloyalty. Disloyalty not only to the person who wronged you, but a disloyalty to God who wants His children to help each other see their own blind defects and crude edges of their character.

Look after each other so that none of you
fails to receive the grace of God.
Watch out that no poisonous root of bitterness
grows up to trouble you, corrupting many.
Hebrews 12:15 NLT

God expresses His Father-way of peace in the Family.

There is not merely a *work* of forgiveness;
there is a *way of life* presented – God's way of following
the process to the blessed end of reconciliation.

One step, the first step, is confrontation . . . if the offender
will permit it.

That God-way of meeting with the offender is not
optional. It is a responsibility before Him and to Him, an
issue of obedience, a mandate . . . not a suggestion. The
Holy Spirit is in charge and directs all.

If your brother sins, go and show him his fault in private;
if he listens to you, you have won your brother.
Matthew 18:15 NASB

A great wonder . . .
Love is the outcome.

A newly intense love and a deeper bond is the blessing,
the union of a secret history kept reverent and clean.
Pleasing to the Father of us both – an increase of His
kingdom over us by the preserving of His Way and Will.

I have seen this many times. The person who is willing to listen, heed and see becomes the dearest of friends in Christ. Grateful for the confrontation, they are delighted in reconciliation with God.

And exuberant joy is the experience of all involved!

Who knows? You could meet your own confrontation. You might discover your own unknowing wrong and get to make it right.

THE WITNESS OF TWO

But if he does not listen to you, take one or two more with you,
so that by the mouth of two or three witnesses
every fact may be confirmed.
Matthew 18:16 NASB

Forgiving is a process, a costly work. When one is offending you, that one is certainly doing the same to others. God's goal is always reconciliation *to Himself!*

The Lord does not abandon one who does not repent and will not see after private confrontation. In the next step, He orchestrates the "two." In the Old Testament, an accusation was established on the testimony of two or three.

If one witness is not heard, then next comes two.
Two victims of the same sin habits
confront the offending one together.

It requires a work together in careful sharing and preparing on bended knee. The Holy Spirit will guide and lead our dealings into God's own view and will.

Two or three prove the accusation and form a bond that can restore the offender . . . if the sinner will hear.

Not just listen, but hear in heart and bow in spirit.
Hear and repent.
Hear and come into God's standard.
Hear and be reconciled to the Father and by that,
                    restored to fellowship and . . . to trust.

SEPARATION

Forgiveness is not the end of forgiving. Beyond forgiving is the work of reconciliation – not to the offended one, but to God!

Many Christians believe that if forgiveness is exchanged then reconciliation must happen. Yet forgiveness and reconciliation are two different issues. There can be forgiveness without restoration of the relationship. I can forgive fully, but if the offender is not changed by sincere repentance, then God might call for a separation.

An offense is a signal.
Something is wrong in obedience,
and the one who cares for God, cares for the sinner.

The sinner's relationship with God becomes the true-forgiver's sacrificial work for the restoration of the offender. The Lord Jesus begins to outline the drastic steps of intervening for the sake of the one He loves, who doesn't love Him.

If he pays no attention to them [refusing to listen and obey],
tell it to the church;
and if he refuses to listen even to the church,
let him be to you as a pagan and a tax collector.
Matthew 18:17 AMP

Old Testament separation was severe for Israel. But New Testament separation is still a clear command to God's people.

Because we have not obeyed the King and
His laws of the Kingdom,
the flock is dirty and sick.

When obedience to the pleasure of the King is the goal, separation from the disobedient is the inevitable result.

The worldly church is full of 'good' and 'nice.' But the Kingdom is full of 'in' and 'out.'

Where the King is allowed to reign, there is division. It is real and practical in Scripture, and the ground of separation is clearly given.

When unity is the goal instead of God's will,
compromise is the glue.

Separation from the rebellious and the spurious
makes for purity of the real Church.

The presence of Jesus' reign in a single life means
wrenching division in all – ALL – the heart-entangled
places. And Jesus promised separation as HIS violent
action on the bowed believer's closest relationships:

*Whoever denies and disowns Me before men, I will also
deny and disown him before My Father Who is in heaven.*

*Do not think that I have come to bring peace upon the earth;
I have not come to bring peace, but a sword.*

*For I have come to part asunder a man from his father,
and a daughter from her mother, and a newly married wife
from her mother-in-law—and
a man's foes will be they of his own household.*
Matthew 10:33-36 AMPC

The willingness to leave those Jesus strikes with His
Knowing Sword is the great test of whether He is truly
King of your affections and Ruler of your relationships.
And the test of your willingness to make yourself odious
in order to to save a sinner's destiny.

There are two places the Dividing Sword falls
to sever relationships.

One is God's strike on our sin of idolatry,
of loving someone more than Him.
The other is the sword swath against relationships
with unrepentant sinners.

SHEEP FOLLOW SHEEP

The rebellious ones who will not come under the King and the false who claim His throne are wolves among the flock and must not be pastured with the sheep.

Sheep are entirely too weak to be in a flock with such dangerous influence.

The innate nature of sheep is to follow sheep.

To their own detriment, sheep will wander astray behind the fearful and the willful. Defiance is highly contagious.

> *He who walks with the wise grows wise,*
> *but a companion of fools suffers harm.*
> *Proverbs 13:20 NIV*

The terms of separation are made plain and simple in scripture. And the Holy Spirit alone applies them in every instance.

The Holy Spirit alone will guide and rule in issues of separation. Neither human reason nor religious legalism should ever decide on division.

Those in Church authority, who agree
on what they have heard and
been shown by the Father,
can instigate separation.

As in Acts, there was prayer first.

ALL ABOUT GOD

Division is never over human relationships. A person is in sin because their walk with God is faulty. Problems with relationships are actually problems with God. Always.

Division is not over doctrine but always over character. Character flaws create doctrinal errors.

To be of 'one mind' is not only a command, it is an easy possibility for the obedient (Romans 12:16, 15:5; Philippians 1:27, 2:2; 1 Corinthians 1:10).

Only together in Christ is unity possible.

SEPARATION IS LOVE

Rejection is unforgiveness,
          but separation – in God's will – is love.

The end result of forgiveness includes the willingness to suffer for the other person's restoration . . . to God!

Division is merely a picture the church portrays of God's own displeasure and His immutable law of consequence.

The Lord's goal in separation is restoration.
          Fatherly discipline, divine chastening—
                    to save us from our stupid folly.

                              And Eternal loss!

The Holy Spirit instigates the separation, and when the Father is satisfied, the separation can end in precious reconciliation with Him and the sweet communion of the saints.

God has given every means of grace and the gift of partaking in His Divine nature. There is no reason for sin to continue to dominate any life.

Division is not cruel. It is saving the spirit from the tyranny of the soul . . .

And it is God's way to use the Church as the agent of His unbending standard and His open door to the repentant.

God's goal is ever the purity of the Church and the sanctity of each believer. If necessary His Father-Heart will not hesitate to use painful measures to secure the complete cleansing of a person's life.

Separation is not to be taken lightly nor instigated without a word from the Father.

Division is excruciating to both sides and only great love will go through it . . .

Love for God—above others, above yourself.

And through His great indwelling Love, we are willing to suffer for the errant brother or sister and at the hands of His fallen child for *His* sake.

The mandate to the offender is to hear.

> *. . . and if he refuses to listen even to the church,*
> *let him be to you as a pagan and a tax collector.*
> Matthew 18:17b AMPC

If confrontation does not bring the repentance of a changed life, then separation is essential.

> **A pagan is one who does not know God**
> **and worships self.**
> **A tax collector is one who does not fear God**
> **and worships money.**

They were the crooks and thieves of Israel. They were outcasts. We are under no obligation to live with such.

Forgiveness creates a glorious bond, but the failure to admit sin is a breach unresolved.

TELL THE CHURCH

The final command if they will not hear? Tell it to the church.

Paul, writing to Timothy, warned him:

> *Alexander the coppersmith did me much harm;*
> *the Lord will repay him according to his deeds.*
> *Be on guard against him yourself,*
> *for he vigorously opposed our teaching.*
> 2 Timothy 4:14-15 NASB

RECONCILIATION IS THE GOAL

The Cross is the proof of God's passion for reconciliation with His creation. We are ministers of reconciliation . . . to God! Not for people as such. Reconciliation with God brings reunion with His children.

Now all these things are from God,
who reconciled us to Himself through Christ
and gave us the ministry of reconciliation, namely,
that God was in Christ reconciling the world to Himself,
not counting their trespasses against them, and
He has committed to us the word of reconciliation.
2 Corinthians 5:18-19 NASB

PEACEMAKERS

A friend once told me,
"The peacemaker is not one who makes peace among believers. A true peacemaker is one who helps others make peace with God!"

Blessed (enjoying enviable happiness, spiritually prosperous–
with life-joy and satisfaction in God's favor and salvation,
regardless of their outward conditions)
are the makers and maintainers of peace,
for they shall be called the sons of God!
Matthew 5:9 AMPC

Lovers of Self

2 Timothy 3:2-5 NIV
People will be lovers of themselves, lovers of money, boastful,
proud, abusive, disobedient to their parents, ungrateful, unholy,
without love, unforgiving, slanderous, without self-control,
brutal, not lovers of the good, treacherous, rash, conceited,
lovers of pleasure rather than lovers of God –
having a form of godliness but denying its power.

Have nothing to do with them.

Paul's letter to Timothy concerns issues in the church, as
to believers. So this shocking account probably refers to
believers! That long list of sin flows from the first issue:

"lovers of self . . ." (v. 2).

The Lover of God will never harmonize with one
whose lover is self. Separation – utter and unequivocal
departure – is the directive.

"Have nothing to do with them" (v. 5).

Love is the great crisis of any life.
Love is the motivation of every life.

What you love determines who you will be.
Your object of love becomes the nature of your identity.
So what you love becomes what you are.

Lovers-of-self worship self by serving and supplying
every soulish whim. So lovers-of-self become inbred
monsters, stealing everything from everyone to feed the
insatiable appetite of Adam for the forbidden fruit.

The reason that worshipers of God cannot and will never experience union in Christ with worshipers-of-self is this:

Lovers-of-self demand the spotlight of the center.
They consume the strengths of the strong,
the gifts of the gifted,
and take the throne from the King.

And the lovers of God, by absolute loyalty to Him, must not and cannot suffer any substitute in His place.

THE LAZY

2 Thessalonians 3:6 AMPC
Now we charge you, brethren, in the name and on the authority of our Lord Jesus Christ (the Messiah) that you withdraw and keep away from every brother (fellow believer) who is slack in the performance of duty and is disorderly, living as a shirker and not walking in accord with the traditions and instructions that you have received from us.

One who is lazy will slip his heavy load into your pocket when you are not aware, and you will find yourself walking weary and stumbling . . . wondering what happened to you.

You will find your own field in weedy disorder while the garden of the lazy blooms.

Sheep cannot bear burdens or pull loads.
Sheep can only sustain their own load of wool.
Nothing more.

It is in this letter to the Thessalonians that Paul makes clear one of the major reasons for separation:

The sloth of one defeats all.

PAUL'S EXAMPLE

Paul was constantly committed to being of no burden to the churches he led, ever setting the example himself of total personal responsibility.

Receiving only from others what he had to, he made it his business to serve. And though he had the highest position as apostle, he never demanded to be served, only followed.

> *For even the Son of Man did not come to be served,*
> *but to serve . . .*
> *Mark 10:45 NASB*

As Paul followed the Master's example, he called the church to follow the same.

> *. . . and when I was present with you and was in need,*
> *I was not a burden to anyone;*
> *for when the brethren came from Macedonia they fully*
> *supplied my need, and in everything I kept myself*
> *from being a burden to you, and will continue to do so.*
> *2 Corinthians 11:9 NASB*

LAZINESS IS WICKEDNESS

The Lord Jesus told a remarkable story called the *Parable of the Talents,* and revealed for all time the cause of fruitlessness.

> *"So I was afraid and went out and hid your talent in the ground. See, here is what belongs to you."*
>
> *His master replied, "You wicked, lazy servant! So you knew that I harvest where I have not sown and gather where I have not scattered seed?"*
> *Matthew 25:25-26 NIV*

What the servant (believer) named understandable fear and careful management,
the Lord called wicked and lazy.

**Laziness is contempt for God
and scorn for His character.
And wickedness is the secret origin of laziness.**

God has the right to expect that His gifts be multiplied for His increase. Multiplication is the nature of the Kingdom and happens through giving all away.

The wicked own God's gifts, but count Him as miserly and hard. The lazy hoard what He gives and so lose all they save.

> *So take the talent from him and
> give it to him who has the ten talents.*
> *Matthew 25:28 ESV*

The Kingdom of God is the great adventure of
responsibility, of tapping the vast wealth of the Kingdom
by obedient generosity.

The lazy, by doing nothing,
     make themselves unfit for Kingdom participation.

The lazy are just another type of lovers-of-self, who by
their neglect and invasion, disturb the Center which
belongs only to the King.

> **The King will not be dethroned.**
> **The Head will not be displaced.**

We are called to fierce devotion,
     not only to the Lord Christ but to His Position.
     And if separation is His calling,
          to defend His Place against usurpers,
          then – no matter the cost –

                              we must separate!

The Torturers

The great crime of the New Testament age is
unforgiveness.

Crime? Yes. Scripture proves it. God considers it a
punishable offense if you have experienced forgiveness
but refuse to give it.

Jesus told a parable to the disciples and children around
Him . . .

A king went to collect a debt owed him by a slave. The
slave owed him 10,000 talents. One talent was worth '15
years wages for a laborer!' The debt was inconceivably
huge and the man could not pay it. So the king was going
to sell him and his wife and children and everything he
had, but the slave fell to the ground and begged.

"Have patience with me and I will repay you everything."
And the lord of that slave felt compassion and released him and
forgave him the debt.

But that slave went out and found one of his fellow slaves who
owed him a hundred denarii (one day's wages); and he seized
him and began to choke him, saying,
"Pay back what you owe."

So his fellow slave fell to the ground and began to plead with
him, saying, "Have patience with me and I will repay you." But
he was unwilling and went and threw him in prison until he
should pay back what was owed.
Matthew 18:26-30 NASB

The king learned about this slave's actions.

Then summoning him, his lord said to him,
"You wicked slave, I forgave you all that debt because you
pleaded with me. Should you not also have had mercy on your
fellow slave, in the same way that I had mercy on you?"
And his lord, moved with anger, handed him over to the
torturers until he should repay all that was owed him.

My heavenly Father will also do the same to you,
if each of you does not forgive his brother from your heart."
Matthew 18:32-35 NASB

I have known and witnessed that this is not a mere story.
It is a fearfully real consequence, and one we don't face or
consider when things go unaccountably bad.

CRIME AND PUNISHMENT

One dear young man gave me the living reality of 'the
torturers.' (I have changed his name and some personal
details to protect his privacy.)

I met Chip through a friend and we became phone pals,
sharing Christ. What Chip shared with me was just the
surface of his story, but it was plenty awful. His father
had abused him in shocking ways and the young man
was badly hurt and confused.

We often talked by phone when he was willing. Mostly I
shared with him who Christ is and what He had taught
me.

Then I didn't hear from Chip again for a couple of years. I
wondered about him but hoped he was all right. One day
he called and told me what had happened to him. He had
suffered a mental breakdown of great darkness, and he
was calling from a facility for the mentally ill.

I listened for some time and then I told him this:
"Chip, you have to forgive your father."

I felt that was the only hope for his life. He was receptive,
but once again I didn't hear from him for many months.

Then one day I heard his voice again on the phone.
"Mrs. Kilpatrick
(He always called me that so respectfully.
He would not call me Martha, he was so dear!),
I want you to know that I am out of the mental hospital
now. I am well and it is all due to you."

"How could that be, Chip?"
Since I hadn't talked to him in so long, I was baffled.

He said, "Do you remember what you told me to do?"
I couldn't recall what I had said that so impacted him,
so he told me. "When I was in the mental hospital, you
told me that the only thing I could do was to forgive my
father."

He paused a moment and said this startling thing.
"The Lord had forgiven me for so much sin, but I would
not forgive my father. So God 'turned me over to the
torturers' and that's when I had a breakdown and
thought I would lose my mind. I spent months in terrible
darkness, and was put in the mental hospital. Then you
told me to forgive. And I did!"

He sounded strong and free and I knew it was the truth.

Chip has told his story as a testimony to the power of forgiveness, so I am free to tell it.

I saw Chip several times over the next few years. He went to the mission field in the Middle East with church backing and a very good mission group. There he had a number of encounters with God's intervening power. One of Chip's stories was an experience of God's miraculous protection. He was on a city bus and he sensed from the Spirit that a certain man had strapped a bomb to himself. He began to pray for God's protection and was asking God what to do. In a very short time, the military stopped the bus and took the man into custody. It was true, he did have a bomb, but they were able to subdue him.

What a story God is telling in Chip's life!

THE MEANING OF OUR SUFFERING

Over the years I have seen many people that seem to have been 'turned over to the tormentors.' The following is a composite story of several people.

A wife simply would not forgive her husband, so she was slowly losing her grip on life. She couldn't function and she lived tormenting her husband and family. I felt she had been turned over to the torturers and I prayed for her.

Finally, God spoke strongly to her and said, "Now is the day. You have to forgive him." Then she did the work to forgive and she came out of her bitterness and into peace.

We need to seek the face of God to understand and discern the meaning of our suffering. Here are eight possibilities from the Scripture:

1. Persecution for Christ's sake. For reward, we rejoice in it (Matthew 5:10-12).

2. The Chastening of God, which is His love, for holiness and peace (Hebrew 12:11). The key is to not despise the chastening of the Lord.

3. Reaping what you sow. *"A man reaps what he sows"* (Galatians 6:7-9). *"Sow to please the Spirit."*

4. Martyrdom, which is a calling from God to which we consent, whether death or suffering in this life (See Stephen, Acts 7).

5. Outright attack of the enemy. Go to prayer and authority (Luke 10:19).

6. Thorn in the Flesh, 'from the devil', used to keep Paul from the danger of pride. *"My grace is sufficient for you"* (2 Corinthians 12:9).

7. Suffer for others. *"So death works in us, but life in you"* (2 Corinthians 4:12).

8. Failure to forgive and so turned over to the torturers (Matthew 18).

Whatever life brings, God's answers are close to you. They are in your spirit and from your Wonderful Counselor, inwardly available to you and ready with your answer.

In all situations, bow your will to God for whatever He is doing and you will receive His life wisdom. You will also become the Light of the World.

I am the light of the world,
He who follows Me will not walk in the darkness,
but will have the Light of life.
John 8:12 NKJV

Glorious Reconciliation

A young woman came to walk with us. She was delightful and had a great love for the Bible. In time, however, it became obvious that there was a religious spirit that caused serious problems and it had to be addressed. One who worked with her told her some very startling things about the affect of her legalism and blindness.

I realized she had a relationship with the Bible but not with the Lord Himself. I asked her to spend some time alone and seek a real relationship with Christ. I told her no one could do that for her. She had to do the work to surrender to Christ herself.

So we entered a period of separation.

She was dear to me and I felt she would come through. She had made such a commitment to Christ in us. She was really my spiritual daughter.

After some months, I suddenly felt free to meet with her. In my spirit, I felt she had experienced a breakthrough. We met for tea, and immediately experienced the joy of reconciliation. She shared her terrible and wonderful journey with me, and I now share it with you, using her own words.

> "I came to see that I had a relationship with my brain and the Book. I would see what someone else had and I would take that and try to perform it. I became a caricature of myself. I created my own identity, and I also made God into what I believed Him to be.

"I sucked the life out of everyone who had something I wanted. I never realized the agony of what that did to others! So I knew I had to have a relationship with Christ. I wouldn't make it otherwise. But I couldn't get to my heart. I had barricaded my heart.

"I had always heard you say, 'It's a choice. Just choose.' But you also said, 'You can choose without **committing** to your choice.' And that was the big answer! I realized I had not committed to my choice to follow Christ.

"There was so much repentance that I felt I would never make it through. I had to have God being God in my life!"

In time, as she shared the profound things the Lord had revealed to her, I was astonished at the depth of His dealings. She called it a 'tsunami of His terrible love,' as our dear Carole often calls it.

I told her, "I wasn't willing to lose you. I held onto Christ and believed you would see Him." And she said, "I wasn't willing to lose you!"

This dear woman had the integrity to love the truth and was willing to be reduced to a desperate need to see the Lord. And He let Himself be found by her. To my Naomi she was a Ruth, who refused to leave even if she was 'left.'

She had to do her own work of seeking the Lord. Alone with God, she began to see her sin, and mostly it was unforgiveness for parents.

This lovely woman accepted responsibility for who she was and what she had done. That is true repentance. This was her scripture:

The Lord is near to all who call upon Him,
To all who call on Him in truth
He will fulfill the desire of those who fear Him.
He will also hear their cry and will save them.
Psalm 145:18-19 NASB

In time she could see it all as Love doing it for Love. Her new person as Christ's follower is delightful, full of joy. And her anointing of the Scripture is always a light to our path.

The Father wants – and has paid for – our reconciliation, but only as we go through the Son.

Christ Himself, being the cornerstone
in whom the whole structure, being joined together,
grows into a holy temple in the Lord.
In him you also are being built together into
a dwelling place for God by the Spirit.
Ephesians 2:20b-22 ESV

Seeing Christ face-to-face must be the foundation of every individual, so that the structure of His dwelling place can be in and among us as . . .

a holy temple in the Lord.

My dear friend offers us this sage advice:
Forgive your parents.
Say thank You.
Tell the truth . . . and
know that it really IS *all about love.*

A Power We Don't Know

Forgiveness is more than a work to do.
It is the power to change the world.

Casting Out the Accuser

The enemy's name is 'accuser of the brethren.' He makes his legal case condemning us continuously, day and night before God. We hear that accusation and we give an answer, either of unconfessed guilt or absolute forgiveness.

Satan goes for the core of Christ's victory:
the absolute forgiveness of the Cross.

The enemy is 'thrown down' by our confident answer. As we forgive and are forgiven, the enemy loses his ground to accuse.

The priceless Blood of the Lamb is the full and final answer to accusation. And Satan is undone.

We forgive our enemies by the same Blood that saved us. That is overcoming Satan on behalf of the one we release and forgive. Our forgiveness ends the enemy's accusation for ourselves and others. It casts the Accuser out.

Now the salvation, and the power, and
the kingdom of our God and the authority of His Christ
have come, for the accuser of our brethren
has been thrown down, he who accuses them
before our God day and night.

And they overcame him because of
the Blood of the Lamb and because of the word
of their testimony, and they did not love their life
even when faced with death.
Revelation 12:10-11 NASB

The testimony is simply this: Jesus Christ is Lord.
That lone declaration shakes loose the enemy's capture
and invasion.

You know. *You know* if you have saved your life to the
losing of your destiny.

To lose your self's centrality is to die, and that is to
overcome fear by the power of love.

God's perfect Love casts out fear.

How to Love Your Enemy

GIVE UP RESENTMENT

Don't fight, don't resist, and don't hate. There is no need when God is in control.

> *Cease from anger and forsake wrath;*
> *Do not fret, it leads only to evildoing.*
> Psalm 37:8 NASB

But there is something you can do.
    Go tell God all you need and want.
    Give thanks in the problem,
        for the very wrong that hurts you so.

Giving thanks is the chance to believe that God is up to something for my good. Imagine! The Peace of God is the reward of meeting Him and the sure promise.

In due time, you will see your God in His perfect justice defend you where you could not defend yourself. You could very well see your enemy become your most committed friend in Christ.

You might even help one be 'snatched from the fire'
    who was headed for hell and death (Jude 23).

And there is something else. What if someone goes to hell because you refused to forgive them, never lifting their burden of guilt so that they could receive God's mercy?

I have been assigned by God's will to many people whose evil focused on me. It was a trust they placed in me by an instinctive knowing they could.

What they are really saying is a desperate,
    "Help me! I am not saved,
        and I will punish you for having God's love
            that I don't have."

This is a calling God places on us all, a calling to endure mistreatment and forgive. Over and over. We can come to the place of letting go of a person's offense so the only thing that matters is their redemption.

Whatever evil they did, I can forgive when I consider an eternity in hell. In comparison, my suffering was nothing.

This is coming to love your enemy: To leave your enormous grievance and fight in prayer for their salvation. It's not about feelings of love, it's about commitment to God – which *IS* love.

Someone who had been badly mistreated once said to me about her abuser, "I don't like her. I am asking God to let me to like her." I replied, "You aren't called to like her but to love her!"

Then she said, "I have been praying so much for her to be saved." And I told her, "That is love!
    To love her eternal destiny
    and to love her enough to pray—
        THAT is love, because it is commitment to
            her and to the Lord."

We have to come to the place where we see the real crisis, not ours, but theirs . . .

and God's unrelenting care for their salvation.

This is good, and it is pleasing in the sight of God our Savior,
who desires all people to be saved
and to come to the knowledge of the truth.
1 Timothy 2:3-4 ESV

True Power, Divine Test

Humanity is power mad, but ignorant of the power of
forgiveness to shake loose the devil's hold on souls.
And! On me.

Forgiveness is power. Earthshaking power.

> Forgiveness is a Divine Test –
> a test of your love for your God.

Forgiveness is a Power and a Test.

The offense makes you seethe with fire to change the
unchangeable, to be heard by the deaf and known by the
blind. The offense spawns in you the drive to control, to
take over as God and force justice and truth into being.

The power of revenge, the dominion of rigid force, the
strength of coercion . . . these are human powers that
tempt the soul against the offender.
> They are sweet to consider,
> > delicious to plot . . .
> > > and deadly to keep.

In forgiveness – true forgiveness – these powers are
forfeited, discarded, and refused along with my "legal
rights" in the situation.

Forgiveness is true power . . .
Forgiveness is the believer's only legitimate power in the
arena of what-is-wrong.

To forgive is to possess holy power on behalf of
      those you are forgiving:
            power to change their lives for God,
            for goodness,
            to free *your* enemy from THE enemy,
               that he might see his error.

In forgiving, as in blessing, you are giving the offender
a gift, the secret gift of freedom from the Legal System,
for Christ's sake, by what He paid. It is a debt of gratitude
you owe Jesus!

Strife and trouble are about God – God in your life, God
in theirs.

      You are not a factor, let alone the central issue.
      Human relationship is entirely secondary.

        **Relationships-on-earth are fixed when
        relationship-divine is solved.**

God, by Pure Design, sends people to offend you that you
might, by Christ, "intercede for the transgressor"
(Is. 53:12).

      The offense is the signal of a need.
      Their need of God. And God's need of them.

Above my issue and overriding my personal pain stands
God's purpose and His glory. His need . . . for Eternity.

      That must be of more concern to me than
          my own petty defense.

Forgiveness is one of the basic calls of the Gospel.

Love is the first call, and when you forgive, you
have access to a love that overwhelms the sinner,
    defeats their enemy,
        and brings God's pleasure to your life . . .

Reigning Grace

While working on the book you hold in your hands, I
wanted to be very clear of any bitterness, so I asked again
for the Lord to show me any unforgiveness in my life.

It seemed I should make a list of those who had been
especially vicious to me, those whose evil had fixated on
me with demonic, irrational fury.

The list was comprehensive, from my girlhood right up to
present day. It was a long list, not surprising for someone
with 77 years of life to ponder!

But when I finished writing down the names and really
looked at the pages, the whole list was shocking because
it represented very great suffering with much agony
and pain. I didn't fully comprehend how great was the
unending stream of evil assault, one person after another,
years on end.

There it was in writing and it became real to me, as
one large, ominous mountain. And with amazement, I
saw that by God's power of His own forgiveness, that
mountain had been cast into the sea.

One person, very sick in soul,
      had planned my murder to look like suicide.
Another dreamed of my death, and in the dream,
      she walked away indifferent to murdering me.
Several people slandered me with awful lies.

I had suffered hate from so many; unnatural, diabolical
hatred that crushed my spirit and broke my heart.

There were many who confessed to a jealousy of me that became a murderous madness, leading them to torment, discredit and try to destroy me.

I believe my life has been a Joseph journey of formation through suffering. The favor of God seemed to be on me, an obvious robe of many colors. But it made me a living target of the haters of God.

It has often been that the people to whom I give the most love and help are the most vicious and bitter in their hatred of me . . .

I was shocked. Could this list really reflect my life? How could one small life be such a target of hell?

But a still greater shock awaited me as I looked at the pages. Over everything and everyone on it, I could see the overwhelming presence of God's GRACE, gentle but oh, so powerful.

Jesus had overcome it all – in me, for me – by the power of Grace, the unearned, unmerited and outlandish favor of God, which is the definition of Grace. Grace supplied all my needs, saving me always from that which was too much and too strong for me.

For out of His fullness
[the superabundance of His grace and truth]
we have all received grace upon grace
[spiritual blessing upon spiritual blessing,
favor upon favor,
and gift heaped upon gift].
John 1:6 AMP

Grace had carried me through every crisis, every crushing. The grace of God had spared my life several times over. I didn't deserve such mercy, such tender care.

He had picked me up when I stumbled,
        cured me of anger,
        comforted me in pain,
        given me love from His children
in place of the persistent hatred that hounded me.

The gifts of His grace were more than I could comprehend and greater than I had ever imagined. Now I could see clearly, I was not left to suffer alone as a victim. He who promised to be with me to the end of time was more THERE than I knew as I lived it.

The great and powerful Grace of God kept me endlessly, to rescue me from enemies but also to save me from my own naiveté and ignorance of evil. I was often a lamb led to the slaughter, and He was faithful to tell me that. He Himself sent me to the slaughter for His own purpose, but He preserved me in it and carried me through to victory.

God's grace enabled me to endure with people, His mercy for me gave me solutions, peace and wisdom beyond me. In ways I never fully saw, His grace was the power to live through all the fires of affliction and emerge without the smell of smoke.

What I read on that list no human could conquer or survive. The only explanation was the tender grace of God, constantly sustaining me, ever protecting me . . . and largely unseen by me.

He gave me the forgiveness for others that He required of me. His grace was kindness and love I didn't deserve, the tender mercies of a Shepherd with a lost and stupid lamb.

Above all, Christ gave me Himself! And I could experience *HIS* sweet love and mercy for the most awful enemy. I was made to see that all suffering was for my good and for my riches in the Spirit. I could freely forgive because I had the GRACE of His undeserved, unearned forgiveness *for me*!

I was ever washed clean of bitterness with my enemies, but also with God Himself. He nurtured me and carried me tight in His arms while I kicked against Him.

Grace is Love beyond the boundaries of belief.

Grace is the expression of an unfathomable, inscrutable compassion that is Christ. He Who loves His haters and cries out for His enemies, lived in me and ruled me. Forgiveness flowed easy as a mountain stream. My need for forgiveness opened that same spring for others. And every day I could bury the list of cruel offenses from my darkest enemy.

For any situation, including those far worse than mine, GRACE is there with a power not human, a power of God's divine nature. Grace is God giving Himself into every unbearable, every injustice.

Paul cried out to be relieved of his 'thorn in the flesh,' but God did not relieve him. Instead He revealed the reason to Paul: the thorn was for his good protection.

God's grace was so powerful that it fully sustained Paul and taught him one of the greatest principles of Life – the power of weakness.

No matter what, God's grace is equal to our suffering . . .

But He said to me, "My grace is sufficient for you,
for power is perfected in weakness."
Therefore, I will most gladly boast
all the more about my weaknesses,
so that Christ's power may reside in me.

So I take pleasure in weaknesses, insults, catastrophes,
persecutions, and in pressures, because of Christ.
For when I am weak, then I am strong.
2 Corinthians 12:9-10 HCSB

Hatred is an insidious Monster, infecting everyone on which it sets its sight. Our only hope in this mad world, this wretched humanity, is the
Grace of God . . .
His compassion, mercy, kindness,
tender care and unfailing love.
He will handle our suffering, preserve our souls,
protect our hearts in secret, and make us rich within
by His quiet, unseen, dynamic power—
called by the soft name of GRACE.

If the world hates you, understand
that it hated Me before it hated you.
John 15:18 HSCB

All through those years as darkness stalked, the Holy Spirit gave an outpouring of insight and revelation to me in teachings and books.

At a Shulamite Ministries conference, *The Road That Leads to Life: The Narrow Way and the Few Who Find It,* my dear sister in the Lord, Rebecca, took me by the hand and said, "I want to show you something."

She led me to the long table of my books and audio series. Still holding my hand, she commanded, "Look at this. You don't know how much God has given you."

As I looked down that long table with stacks of audio series and books, I wept at the wonder of it. All THAT came through ME from Christ?

She pointed to different series and could tell me what was going on in her life that those messages addressed. And I was as overwhelmed as she knew I would be, to see what light Christ had produced during those 'dark nights of the soul.' Life was winning over darkness despite me, and God was using me . . . again by His grace and mercy.

The following scripture became my life verse years ago. It was given to me often by two I call family, Don and Carole.

> *I will give you the treasures of darkness*
> *And hidden wealth of secret places,*
> *So that you may know that it is*
> *I, The LORD, THE GOD OF ISRAEL,*
> *WHO CALLS YOU BY YOUR NAME.*
> *Isaiah 45:3 NASB*

It has assured me that there was rich meaning in my dark times, even "treasures in that darkness, a hidden wealth of secret places!"

GOD LONGS FOR US TO COME TO GRACE.

The Father looks on us all as depraved Prodigals,
    wallowing in the black pit of sin's shame.

He waits and watches and plans outlandish grace,
    inconceivable to human logic.

We can resist Grace and reject the Giver.
We can prefer the enemy's whisper that
    defends us, accuses God, and blames 'them.'
    We can do that, but
        **GRACE is God's goodness on the move,
        and He will keep coming!**

After contemplating the list of forgiven enemies, I set out to make another list. God's kindness and sovereign power sent to me vessels of His grace.

They loved me and encouraged me,
they stood for me and nurtured me in my broken heart.
Their prayers sustained me and healed me.
They showed me God's heart for me and
displayed His own grace by their patience and fidelity.

The list is long and precious. God alone knows how they were His vessels of that wondrous Grace.

God sent them,
>   God indwelt them,
>>   and He also holds their reward,
>>>   a vast debt I could never pay.

Our God reigns on a Throne of *GRACE!* He rules above all things by the mighty transcendence of grace. He lavishes grace on us, His children.

Grace is so abundant that we could never exhaust its supply.

The danger is to fail to come boldly to that throne for
>   the power of grace to live this life,
>>   in the fellowship of Christ's sufferings.

Therefore let us draw near with confidence
to the throne of grace, so that
we may receive mercy and find grace
to help in time of need.
Hebrews 4:16 NASB

Refusing to Forgive

You are free to not forgive.
Absolutely your choice . . . but you will not
be free of guilt, anguish, or punishment.

Hamlet, Revenge and Power

Some time ago, I watched Mel Gibson's excellent *Hamlet* again, and suddenly I saw the real story for the first time. The story is a perfect picture of the devastation of revenge.

Never take your own revenge, beloved,
but leave room for the wrath of God, for it is written,
"VENGEANCE IS MINE, I WILL REPAY," says the Lord.
Romans 12:19 NASB

The story is this: Hamlet's father-king is murdered by his own brother, with poison administered into his ear. The murderer then marries Hamlet's mother a mere two months later, taking over the throne of Denmark. No one in the kingdom suspects that it was murder. However, the dead king appears to Hamlet as a ghost (seeming to rise from hell) to tell him how his death occurred and to demand that Hamlet take revenge for his murder. Hamlet is filled with horror and grief. But he now has the dilemma of whether to avenge the death.

The famous "to be or not to be" speech
is actually Hamlet's agony of choice.

The evil he has discovered is an unbearable continuing presence in his world, and he longs to escape by suicide but he is too afraid to kill himself, not knowing what lies on the other side of death.

So he is left with a major decision. Will he let the whole thing just be, doing nothing about it, or shall he take revenge as the "ghost" demands?

"To be or not to be"—that really is question of us all.
But it could be better stated this way:
"To be or not to be . . . *God.*"

Revenge plays God and takes the sword of punishment out of His Hand.

All of us will ask the question and ALL of us will make the choice whether to seek revenge or not.

Agony of choice. This is a near madness for Hamlet.
Torn by the death of his beloved father, horrified at his mother's infatuation with her new husband, he behaves irrationally – as a mad man – but will not tell anyone the secret of his predicament.

Revenge is just such a burning torment.
It is rage capable of murder.
Filled with the passion of reckless acts,
it sweeps the guilty, but also the innocent,
into its maelstrom.

Hamlet's lust for vengeance damages everyone in his path . . . *everyone.*

Hamlet's fury is transferred to the woman he loves, his fiancée, Ophelia. He deliberately tortures and mocks her. She is utterly bewildered, believing that she is his problem.

Ophelia, the innocent, bears all the scorn Hamlet would have loved to pour on his mother and his vile stepfather.

Ophelia is forced to bear the anguish of Hamlet's hatred.

Retaliation consumes him and even his loves are turned into hatred by bitterness. In the bloodthirsty obsession of bitterness, Hamlet punishes most the one he loves the best – the one who loves him and who deserves it least.

**Malice always seeks out the most vulnerable
to satisfy a thirst for violence.**

As Hamlet sets out to murder his stepfather and punish his mother, there were many deaths as a direct result of his revenge.

- Two friends are executed in England by Hamlet's arrangement.

- Ophelia's father is killed by Hamlet.

- Ophelia, driven mad by it all, takes her own life by drowning (the only one not killed by the sword or poison, she commits suicide in bewildered grief).

Ophelia's brother then challenges Hamlet to a duel and puts deadly poison on his sword so that even the slightest cut will kill Hamlet. By events born of that duel,

- The queen-mother dies from poison intended for Hamlet.

- Ophelia's brother dies (by his own poison).

- The evil king is forced to drink his own poison, and at last . . .

- Hamlet himself dies, by a mere scratch from the poisoned sword.

Revenge is deadly poison.

The one who takes up the sword of revenge will eventually drink his own poison and die by his meddling hand.

**Revenge is death to the avenger . . .
not only the offender.**

Ironically, seizing revenge that belongs only to God is certain suicide.

Eight people are swept into unnecessary death for the cause of Hamlet's revenge, six of whom are not only innocent but also ignorant of the evil murder.

In the end, Hamlet was far more evil than his stepfather, eight times the murderer his enemy was. In his mania of revenge, he destroyed everyone he loved, from friends and fiancée to his mother. And finally, even himself.

**Bitterness is a madness, yes, but it is
also a bloodthirsty violence,
taking the innocent down with it.**

I personally believe that the "ghost" represents Satan, appearing always in disguise, ever whispering in the dark, inciting rage, building a legal case against the guilty – sometimes with fact, more often with falsehood. He demands that we be the arbiters of justice because there is none due to God's inaction, ever arguing strongly for us to take matters into our own hands. To be 'God.'

The subtle inference, old as Eden:
"God isn't doing anything about it
and doesn't love you enough to care."

To be or not to be . . . God!

Hamlet.
A frighteningly real picture of revenge . . .
and very true to life.

There were three choices for Hamlet:
    To die himself,
    to simply let it be,
    or to kill the guilty.

He did not consider another alternative,
    the only solution of peace:
    his own soul-death.
Dying to his rights – by giving up to God his rage and
power and simply leaving it all with Him.

Had Joseph used the sword of vengeance, he would
never have ruled over Egypt's riches. Had Daniel chosen
revenge, he would have ended early on as lion food.

Beloved, revenge is not mine.
Nor yours.
It belongs to God.

For we know Him who said,
"Vengeance is Mine, I will repay."
And again, "The Lord will judge His people."
Hebrews 10:30 HSCB

> *"Vengeance is Mine, and retribution,"*
> *in due time their foot will slip; for*
> *the day of their calamity is near, and the*
> *impending things are hastening upon them.*
> Deuteronomy 32:35 NASB

REVENGE AND POWER

Unforgiveness holds a certain heady power – the right to revenge – even if only secret hating and silent pouting. To give up that sweet hatred is to relinquish your power, however big or small, over the offender.

It is hard to do . . . because IF you forgive and let it go, then you are left completely defenseless. Totally helpless against one who has already violated you.

And IF you forgive, that one will suffer no penalty,
　　　　no loss, no consequence
　　　　　　　　unless God takes up your revenge and . . .
He might not do anything for a long, long . . . *long* time.

　　　　　"If I leave it with God,
　　maybe I can't trust Him to attack my enemy."

　"Knowing God, He might overlook the whole thing!
　　　　　　　If I forgive."

　　"If I forgive, I forfeit all power over the person
to deny him (or her) a blessing. Also, I take the risk
that the person will never see the wrong and never be
　　　held accountable for it in this life."

Revenge wants action NOW.
And that is itself evidence of revenge,
    the impatience to make the offender SEE and pay.

Being an older woman, I have had numerous people take
their hate for a mean mother out on me. More than once
I have said to someone, "You are trying to murder your
mother. And I am not the one who hurt you."

One very honest mother told me she realized she had
poured out her revenge against a harsh, cruel father on
her children.

This is not a rare thing! The only rarity is a mother who is
willing to see it, repent, and ask forgiveness.

Or a husband, his wife. A boss, his workers.

When we don't forgive from the heart, we will find
someone to punish. The only thing we don't count on is
that it inevitably will shoot us in the back!

Not to mention it draws God's wrath.

Pride Is

Most hurt is the pain of pride, for which there is no relief but humility. Very few hurts are actually "suffering for Christ" (Col. 1:24).

Pride is . . . being more important than Jesus.

Pride is . . . being in love with "self" more than with God.

Pride is . . . wanting to "feel good" more than desiring God's will.

Pride is . . . caring more for temporary matters than for eternal permanence.

To be misunderstood is excruciating,
but only to dignity.

Being maligned is intolerable,
but only to self-worship.

Denied esteem is traumatic,
but only to ambition.

Persecution is disabling,
but only to the rebellious.

Anger is tempting but only to the selfish.
    Bitterness is caressed only by the vain.
        Revenge is calculated only by the rebel.

    Hatred is indulged only by the wicked.

And Pride will never . . . *ever* forgive.
And so, can never be forgiven.

Bitterness Is

*Exercise foresight and be on the watch to look [after one
another], to see that no one falls back from and fails to secure
God's grace (His unmerited favor and spiritual blessing),
in order that no root of resentment
(rancor, bitterness, or hatred)
shoots forth and causes trouble and bitter torment, and
the many become contaminated and defiled by it . . .[1]
Hebrews 12:15 AMPC (emphasis mine).*

Bitterness is . . . hurt cherished past sundown and
becomes the nest that devils dig in your soul to infect
your whole being with Satan's own rage toward God.

Bitterness is . . . pain twisted into malice,
                              injustice turned to legalism,
                                       sin changed into evil.

Bitterness is . . . unforgiveness that thrusts a root into
your heart from which a spontaneous evil grows
            and becomes the caustic fruit of your life.
            Then ingested by all your world.

Bitterness is . . . a stage on which the devil can rehearse
the scenes of your injustice
            and you can sit in the audience,
            reviewing the pictures and words,
                        remembering, remembering . . .
                        over and over,
                                    hating and hating more . . .

Bitterness is . . . a disease of the soul
    that turns into literal poison and
    infects your own body with sickness and worse –
        infects the world with your hate.

When you fail to forgive the offender, you *become* the
offender yourself.
    You, now the guilty, instead of the other.

And your oppressor has turned into your victim, with the
same measure of offense against you that you had with
him . . . perhaps more.

Bitterness takes root when you believe you are above the
Most High God – more "just" than God, more "good"
than Jesus, and more "able" than the Spirit (Is. 14:12-14).

   Bitterness sprouts and grows from the dirt of pride.

The arrogance of "I would *never* do what you did" and
the egotism that scorns the offender as worthless.

---

[1] A "root of bitterness" in Hebrews 12:15 means a wicked person whose
life and behavior is now offensive to God and obnoxious to men (Strong's
#4088). In a moral sense to be polluted or corrupt (Strong's #3392).

The Unoffended

The most rare and shocking thing you could ever meet
is someone who walks every step
in Jesus' joyful forgiving.

Expectations Lead to Offenses

Some years ago, I was just going about my duties. As I remember it, I was bending over a bag of groceries in the car and I heard God speak to me, "Have no expectations of anyone on earth. Expect only of Me."

"Ah," I thought. "What a wise word! I will do that." Now many years later, I am still learning to "do" it, by the frequent failure at it!

That simple command – "have no expectations" – probably strikes at the heart of the Adamic nature. The core of our ruined humanity to presume that what we want of other people is what they should give . . . be . . . do. The "I-am-god" nature.

When you are disappointed in a person, do you forgive them their failure? Not yet. You first ask forgiveness for having expectations.

Expectations are a waiting pit, an open grave of your own digging, that trips you for a long plunge into bitterness.

Humanity cannot be trusted.
Humanity cannot be holy.
The Cross proves it.

If our best and highest human goodness is nothing but foul and smelly rags, fit only of death (Is. 64:6), then how can we have any expectations of anyone?

To understand that "I cannot do what I want to do" (Romans 7) is to comprehend that no one else can either, apart from the Life that Saves (Romans 8).

If I can do nothing, how wrong is it to expect anyone else to do right?

When I expect my own idea of what a person should do or be, I am setting myself up to be offended, not so much by the person's failure but by my own expectations!

When I do not (as Jesus) "believe" in humanity, then I am not going to struggle unendingly with forgiveness.

**Where there are no expectations,
there are no offenses.**

**Where there are no offenses,
there is no need to forgive.**

So much of the struggle to forgive is merely my own sin of "faith in man," who is utterly corrupt in heart and cannot change himself!

My expectations of *you* are entrapment, a 'noble' attempt to control for selfish reasons and therefore cruel. *You* are God's problem and His responsibility.

Your expectations of *me* are a snare, a cruel distraction from my Focus, who alone can be His own faithfulness WITHIN me.

FREE TO CHOOSE

God's great gift – the measure of His love – is full and total freedom of choice.

> Each of us is free to choose God, or reject Him.
> Free to be evil in Satan or good in Christ.

Entanglement happens when we wrestle with another person's choice of darkness and choose the light for them, against their will. Or struggle with a person's choice of Light to drag them into our beloved darkness.

Entanglement happens when we want the praise of men more than the praise of God . . . and work for it (John 5:44; 12:43)!

Jesus watched the rich young ruler with love, so much love that He would not interfere with his willful choice, deadly though it was (Matthew 19:22).

NO NEED TO FRET

I learned a great wisdom in Israel. I was on a tour with two friends. We were a bus of about 40 people, strangers to each other. As we journeyed from one site in Jerusalem to another, one of the tourists was always late to the bus. And 39 of us had to wait for her to arrive.

This happened every time. She had no regard for us, only for what she decided to see. She held to no schedule and seemed oblivious that it was rude to all of us.

People were getting increasingly frustrated and it was affecting our enjoyment of the journey. I started to silently fume and fret. I asked the Lord to do something about it.

He said to me, "Is this your responsibility?"

I was astonished at the idea and realized that I did not have any responsibility there, to the group or to anyone. The guide and driver had the responsibility and the authority. And they were doing nothing about it. They simply waited. If we were made late to our next site, it wasn't mine to fret.

It seemed the Lord said,
"Sit back, read your Bible,
and have your own time with Me."

And then I heard this,
"Don't become so involved that you have to forgive."

I was amazed. Don't take up an offense that isn't important, so then you won't have to work to forgive. I was free. I submitted to the decision of the authority. I simply accepted her and then I sat back in my seat and enjoyed the ride or – as it still happened – the wait.

Everyone was frustrated and resentful of this woman. I was no longer offended with her so I engaged a little with her at supper when she happened to sit across from me. I was happy and free and I laughed a lot. She laughed with me.

She said, "Oh, I haven't laughed like this in years. "

That was the signal of a tragic life. She was a very unhappy woman even though she knew Christ.

The Holy Spirit was moving and now my attitude wasn't quenching Him. I began to experience God's mercy and love for her. Nothing else was as important. Soon I could discern she had suffered in life, and she was dark and miserable. Christ in me knew this and gave me grace to be friendly. And I prayed a lot for her after that, but I never prayed she would stop keeping us waiting.

I don't know what impact this episode had on her. But I believe that God touched her as He wanted to and – for once – I had not hindered Him by some petty frustration.

LITTLE

To forgive, you must be "little." Only "little" people forgive.

> It costs to forgive. It costs to not-forgive.
> Either way, the price is high
> for the only life you have.

Offenses are a great spiritual crisis, but they usually are not an emergency. Your relationship with God is at stake. The gate to His presence is legally locked against the one who refuses to forgive.

Your destiny is on trial,
> your divine purpose is on the line
> > and therefore your eternity.

Life and death are in the balance – spiritual and physical.

No offense is worth the price of losing your Personal Father, your life's glory, your eternal destiny . . . and! your present peace.

Let go and put on the heart of Christ,
to be Himself in you . . .

So, as those who have been chosen of God, holy and beloved,
put on a heart of compassion, kindness, humility,
gentleness and patience; bearing with one another, and forgiving
each other,
whoever has a complaint against anyone;
just as the Lord forgave you, so also should you.
Colossians 3:12-13 NASB

GOD'S EXPECTATIONS

Watchman Nee said, "God has no expectations of you for He knows you can do nothing. He expects only of His Son." Nee also said that the only thing God requires of man is to tell the truth, and of that we are capable.

This is the brilliant simplicity of the Shepherd with His small sheep.

Trust in God Alone

Now while He was in Jerusalem at the Passover Feast
many people saw the miraculous signs
He was doing and believed in His name.

But Jesus would not entrust Himself to them,
for He knew all men.

He did not need man's testimony about man,
for He knew what was in a man.
John 2:23-25 NIV

For all His love and grace, for all His profound
relationships, still Jesus did not 'entrust' Himself to
anyone. Even if they believed utterly in His name.

The *New King James* and the *King James* translate 'entrust'
as *"commit Himself."*

The *Amplified Bible* reads, *"Jesus (for His part) did not trust*
Himself to them."

The *New American Standard Bible* says, *"Jesus on His part,*
was not entrusting Himself to them."

The Greek word for "trust" here is *pisteuo,* and it means
"to believe, to place confidence in, to trust, reliance upon"
(Strong's #4100). John used this word far more than any
other gospel – 99 times. It is often translated "believe."

The Biblical word "believe" implies that you give *your*
being into that which you believe is true. It is much more
than just mental assent to a truth.

It is the transfer of your very self, of your entire being, giving yourself over – and into – the object of your belief.

Jesus did not give Himself over to any person.

He did not rely on anyone. He did not "trust" even those who exuberantly believed in Him. It was not a cynical despair but the simple reality of two fundamental things.

One, humanity is a fallen race, totally untrustworthy, and corrupt. The best and the worst are equally and totally fallen. You cannot give yourself to that which cannot possibly keep you.

Two, Jesus was given – utterly and completely – to His Father, and God had exclusive and inclusive rights of total access to Jesus and complete ownership of His Son.

No human being had control or influence over Jesus. He tolerated no such enmeshment and no such interference.

Jesus had one allegiance.
One relationship.
One Master and one Lord.

And He commanded us to live in the same chosen boundary of God's ownership . . .
absolute and unequivocal.

Permitting no rival and no distraction, not even allowing anyone's participation in the secret place of that Divine relationship.

Jesus' habit was to spend nights alone with God in the bleak mountains of Israel . . . a picture of the privacy of His intimacy with the Father. No disciple was invited or permitted to enter that secret "tent of meeting."

No description is written about Jesus' night vigils, no information, no pattern revealed. All of it was secret and remains secret.

> Was it prayer?
> Was it worship?
> Silence?

Not even one second of it is revealed.
> That communion is left to our personal discovery,
> our own visit to the mountain trysts during
> the dark and silent hours of earth's natural sleep.

We believers are entirely too dependent on humanity.

We are too much enmeshed with a humanity that cannot be the support of our hopes or a source of our dependence. And who can live up to our expectations of fidelity? So our offenses are deep and intensely wounding.

Our disappointment in betrayal is devastating, not over the offense, but because our own foolish trust and illegitimate bonds are so violated.

Love – God's agape – does not mean trusting a person to bear you up, to understand you, to sustain you.

These are God's roles for which He is extremely Jealous!

Real love is giving, not leaning—
    freedom, not chains of attachment.

Love is setting others entirely free of the burden *of you*.
Giving them space to fly or fail without the load of your
heavy expectation.

**The stake of your life's success depends on
no other person . . . only yourself and your God.**

Jesus loved fiercely. He had profound compassion.
He gave His very life for the love of God for humanity.
    But He never gave His soul's secrets,
        nor the responsibility for His journey,
            to any other person.

For love, He gave His Throne,
He gave His life's blood.
He even gave up His Father's presence on the Cross.

But He never gave His private soul into the hands of
Adam and Eve's unworthy children . . .

Jesus' forgiveness flowed easily and constantly
                by the open absence of expectations.

Disentangled Soldier

Take [with me] your share of the hardships
and suffering [which you are called to endure] as
a good (first-class) soldier of Christ Jesus.

No soldier when in service gets entangled in the enterprises
of [civilian] life; his aim is to satisfy
and please the one who enlisted him.
2 Timothy 2:3-4 AMPC

Paul called his young disciple to accept the sufferings of association with Jesus, to accept them not as a good and noble Christian, but as a *"soldier of Christ Jesus."*

We Christians are in a war.

We live in a foreign land, conquered but still terrorized. The enemy is defeated but he is on the loose. His is an underground covert operation and we are the defenders of the peace our Captain has secured.

We stand as Watchmen for the rights of our King.

Satan is powerless if we use our power of authority and faith, but the problem is recognizing him. The enemy is a sneak. He hides in evil shadows and uses wrongdoings to separate us, not only from each other but from God!

We get swallowed up in pains, absorbed with wounds, lost in lust for personal vindication. And then we are fallen soldiers—out of the ranks, useless to the Captain, often suffering from Band-Aid injuries and treating them as amputations.

If we understood this life as war,
with an enemy attack waiting at every bend in the road,
we wouldn't be so touchy.

Always caught off guard and rarely prepared for battle,
we believers wrestle and struggle with the inevitable pain
of this life. Much of our struggle is 'against' rather than
'for.'

**Seldom do we see that behind the strife and
underneath the bitterness is the diabolical Lucifer.
He has used a human shield, in the guise of a person,
to spew his attack . . . to topple the warrior.**

We are in the middle of a war. The war is not to
determine the winner, but to undergird the accomplished
victory. The war is not against our character or
reputation. Not about our hurt feelings or losses.

The war is launched to disrupt our bond to the Captain
(through unforgiveness), our restful relationship with
God from which all abundance flows and out of which
His own purpose is realized.

Though we can be wounded and even severely injured,
we are called to be disentangled with
the affairs of this world –
occupied not with the wars of earth
nor even of the heavens
but with the Glorious Ruler.

Engrossed with our Mighty Captain.

His pleasure, not ours.
His glory, not yours.
His plan, not mine.

We have a perfect Captain, already victorious. His wishes and His pleasure are to be our life's highest joy and our consuming interest.

Any skirmish, any wound that takes the mind and heart from that One focus is entanglement with the world.

Energy – and precious time – poured out on strife and worries is entanglement with the world.

Let us gaze long at our Captain in His quiet dignity.
From quarrels and attacks,
He simply walked away . . .

Always and only absorbed with His Father's agenda,
He would not be . . . trapped.

Jesus let the strife be.
He let the talkers talk, the fighters fight.
And He let the accusations fly.

Jesus concerned Himself, simply and totally, with God's will and God's orders . . . splendid and utterly fascinating. Plans too wonderful to stop for human folly of fights and rights.

For God called you to do good, even if it means suffering,
just as Christ suffered for you. He is your example,
and you must follow in his steps.
He never sinned, nor ever deceived anyone.
He did not retaliate when he was insulted,
nor threaten revenge when he suffered.
He left his case in the hands of God,
who always judges fairly.
1 Peter 2:21-23 NLT

Though Jesus sometimes answered His accusers,
He did so on His own terms, not theirs.
More often He gave them grilling questions instead of
the answers they demanded.

He was never subject to their terms of arguing, and the
debate ended when HE ended it.

. . . they sought again to seize him,
but He escaped out of their hand.
John 10:39 NKJV

When Jesus had finished
these words, He departed . . .
Matthew 19:1 NASB

Entanglement, with situations and persons,
is the struggle sure to defeat the soldier . . .
and certain to inflict open wounds that require
the tedious stitching of
repentance and forgiveness.

A good first-class soldier's "code of non-entanglement" might be this:

> I am not involved in any activities of mankind;
> they have no reality.
>
> I am not embroiled with any "human" quarrels;
> they have no reality.
>
> I am not entrapped in any worldly ambitions;
> they have no reality.
>
> I am not enmeshed with any "human" relationships;
> they have no reality.
>
> I am in Union with Christ, who alone IS Reality,
> and His Will, the only worthy focus.

ONE RABBI, ONE FATHER, ONE TEACHER

Strange restriction was given to Jesus' disciples toward the end of His life. A limitation in relationship, one we have not heard, much less obeyed.

> *But you are not to be called 'Rabbi,' for you have
> only one Master and you are all brothers.*
> *Matthew 23:8 NIV*

Let no one give you the responsibility for their spiritual growth. That is entanglement.

> *And do not call anyone on earth 'father,'*
> *for you have one Father and He is in heaven.*
> Matthew 23:9 NIV

Give no one the responsibility for your childlike need of a parent. The only one who can father you is the Father in Heaven. To have an earthly 'father' is . . . entanglement.

> *Nor are you to be called 'teacher,'*
> *for you have one Teacher, the Christ.*
> Matthew 23:10 NIV

Only One Teacher can teach you in a perfect and individual instruction. Your Teacher will speak to you through His vessels and you will recognize His Voice always . . . when it is your custom to live hearing more than thinking, listening more than telling.

Let no one teach you, and be the teacher of no one. God's voice and instruction can come through any human vessel, but only His voice, the quickening of the Holy Spirit to me, constitutes His teaching.

Anything else is . . . entanglement.

One Rabbi. One Father. One Teacher. One relationship. One dependency.

Anything added to that is . . . entanglement.

The strength of the Christian's life is precisely the measure of his solitary relationship in seclusion with God. The measure of his worth to the Body of Christ is the same.

Individual intimacy alone with the Father, Rabbi, and
Teacher is one type of dynamic. Add one more servant
of Jesus and you have church – an entirely different
operation of fellowship with the Divine. Church is two or
more who belong utterly to Christ, who meet for focusing
on Him together. That is heaven on earth . . .

Both relationships are essential . . .
    yet church functions only out of, only from,
        the secret fountain of the One Relationship.

DEAD AND UNTOUCHABLE

*Therefore we have been buried with Him through baptism into
death, so that as Christ was raised from the dead
through the glory of the Father,
so we too **might walk in newness of life.**
For if we have become united with Him
in the **likeness of His death,** certainly we shall also be
in the **likeness of His resurrection,***

*knowing this, **that our old self was crucified with Him,**
in order that our body of sin might be done away with,
so that we would no longer be slaves to sin;
for he who has died is freed from sin.
Romans 6:4-8 NASB (emphasis mine)*

When I was baptized by immersion, I understood that it
represented my burial, the real and actual death of my
old life – dead, buried in Christ. When I came up out of
the water, I could completely 'reckon myself dead' and
live that as true.

Shortly after, someone said something cruel and I
thought, "Well, that can't hurt a dead woman."
And sure enough, it never touched me, moved me,
or hurt me.

I have failed, again and again, to remain dead.
It is one of the most difficult issues (for me) to believe.
"I act alive! How can I be dead?"
I am continually reminded that
the old self MUST be dead.
I can't bear her!

The only remedy for sin and failure is
to "believe myself dead" as a **fact**.

Even so, consider yourselves to be dead to sin
[and your relationship to it broken], but alive to God
[in unbroken fellowship with Him] in Christ Jesus.
Romans 6:11 AMP

There is no other way to live, than to be
dead to self and alive to God.

This is to be truly disengaged from everything
that wants to entangle you!

The Strange Humility of Jesus

So Jesus answered them by saying,
I assure you, most solemnly I tell you,
the Son is able to do nothing of Himself
John 5:19 AMPC

There is no encountering humility in humanity.
There is inferiority, acquiescence, oppression.
Self-effacement and laziness . . . but not humility.

All these are covered-up qualities of arrogance.
Weird self-focus, seemingly the opposite side of pride,
      is still pride . . . not the deep modesty
            that is the inherent nature of Christ.

Humility is Jesus' very self, His innate nature.

The opposite, Pride, is humanity's corruption from Eden,
the obsessive focus of self.

      So to gaze at Jesus' strength and forcefulness,
      His perfect calm . . . is not to understand humility
            but to be mystified by it.

We stand void and ignorant before the humility of Christ.

Jesus' humility is entirely strange to normal humanity.
He stands as an alien presence to our world of egoism
gone mad.

He is consummate smallness
pouring forth exceptional greatness.
      We are lost as to how to be like Him,
           nor do we really want to be because . . .

We would have His greatness, but not His nothingness.
We lust for His dominion, but never His surrender.
We desire His acclaim, but reject His rejection.
We want His grand speaking,
      but we are opposed to His odd silence.

Humility is divine and only Jesus possesses it,
      manifests it, and defines it.
           He is the walking humility of God.
           True humility is the attribute of Christ only.
      We have never seen it before He came.

We have seen brokenness – in Joseph, David, Jacob,
           Mary Magdalene . . .

But we have never seen a nature born in
         such purity of humility
         as to exhibit superiority to no one:
         not the woman at the well,
         the tax collector, the prostitute.

Our Lord Jesus Christ is
    utterly void of the pride that is our primal nature
        and toward which we are so tolerant.

He presumes no opinion, He waits to hear.
He offers no reason for His way,
    allows Himself to be assessed by fools.

He is humble enough to be fully Himself,
    to name His real name,
    to respond with naked truth . . .
    and to walk His own path
    without diversion, approval or influence.

He accepts no pressure
    and shies from no conflict.

    Such strength of purpose
        we would not call humble.
    We would label such resistance to control
        an arrogance of the first order.

Nor would we commend His blazing encounters (Mt. 23),
    His rude behavior, His bluntness,
        His cavalier dismissal of family (Mk. 3).

Proof that we know nothing of humility.

The best of us must feign humility
    or walk in inner worthlessness
    and call it humble.

Christ's sacrificial surrender to the Father
is a compelling force residing inside you
    and - if you will - steeping you in the
    very nature of His selfless love.

To know His meekness, you must experience it
    from within, from His Life responding to
    your dilemmas and letting you taste
    His selfless nature, His utter servanthood.

Jesus is still laying down His life, His reputation,
    His rights and doing so with peculiar humility.
        Only now, He does so within His disciples.

You do not *see* it, you do not *understand* it.

You live the humility of Christ knowing
    it is nothing of you,
        nothing from you.

    You live the shocking un-ambition of Jesus
    in the full knowledge that never, ever
        could you be as He is.

That low. That small. That selfless.

His humility is not something to copy.
It can never be done. Not by anyone.

Jesus' very Being is humility: an absence of pride
        unheard of, unseen, unimagined!
That humility – as Christ Himself – lives in believers,
        longing to be valued and released.

This meek Christ stands humbly as
        the Lowly Sentinel of our soul,
        waiting, ready, sufficient for the one who is finally
            sickened by the relentless pride
            that ever pets and promotes its Self.

Christ's humility simply appears in the one who lives in
and by His presence. Being the gift of Himself,
the lack of vanity is the only solution to
        the inherent Adamic flaw of pride.

And . . . Jesus' strange humility is the ultimate power to
break proud humanity.

Living Forgiving

You are forgiven in an unbroken river of grace
that flows through the stream of your life.

A Living Sacrifice

The "Way of Christ" is a life hidden within a constant
flow of forgiveness, walking inside the gift of His Cross
through every step, in every situation. Ever conscious
of His Sacrifice, living under the shadow of the Bloody
Cross and never leaving it.

**Forgiveness is not a now-and-then event;
it is a very lifestyle that issues from worship,
from adoration of the Savior.**

The highest potency of forgiveness lies within the
framework of worship and prayer. Worship is, above all,
surrender to lie voluntarily on an altar of sacrifice out of
love for Christ, who laid Himself there for me and for all.

Incense in the Holy Place burned always, unendingly.
The incense stands for prayer, constantly offered, day and
night.

The Altar of Sacrifice is to
*"present your bodies, a living and holy sacrifice,
acceptable to God,
which is your spiritual service of worship"*
(Romans 12:1 NASB).

Yet . . . there was no fragrance rising to God's pleasure, no
wafting smoke, without a fire. A smoldering fire, burning
always, never dying out. No visible flame, just a hidden
glowing. An unending aroma flowed from a tiny fire ever
rising to God's presence.

The scent of the offering . . . this is prayer,
and the willingness to burn is forgiveness.

A living sacrifice we are and must be, ever offering ourselves up for the burning of "selfish flesh" on the altar.

That is what offenses do . . .

They expose our self-worship
        and enflame the touchy self that
            demands all situations support our ego and ease.

A flame is ignited when we are wronged and burns either to bitter rage or to the smoldering end of the soul's greed for revenge.

Many will bear Jesus' name, some will live for Him, and some will even die for Him, but few are the "living sacrifices" offered for perpetual death to be the focus of humanity's violent hatred of God.

A surrender unto death – that is our worship.

**Many will bear His cross;
few will be His living sacrifice.**

Prayer is not at all about words.

Prayer is a life voluntarily laid on the altar of death and ignited to burn deep within its being, bearing the offenses of Christ's outright enemies and . . . His disloyal friends. This is

> . . . *filling up what is lacking in Christ's afflictions.*
> *Colossians 1:24 NASB*

Something far above just the normal forgiveness work, so beyond my own issue and self. There is a profound meaning, a vicarious redemption going on in my suffering. It is:

"I bear on my body the brand-marks of Jesus."
Galatians 6:17 NASB

A mysterious suffering for the salvation of souls, sharing the agony of Christ for sinners. It is not about me. The issue is not my rights nor my personal pain.

Christ and His need—
this is the pinnacle of forgiveness.

To touch Christ's purpose and His suffering above your personal pain is to suddenly see inside the very agony of Jesus over humanity's willful self-worship and then . . . enter His heart of radical, opulent forgiveness.

Jesus uses our offered body,
> our rolling agony,
> the soul's silent dying,
> to play out the drama of mankind's pathetic need.

Accepting the offenses and offering them up to His Holy Lordship, who alone can bear and take them.

Bind the festival sacrifice with cords
to the horns of the altar.
Psalm 118:27 NASB

This is incense . . .

Prison Breakout

I once read an unusual story about the power of forgiveness. A convent needed more buildings, so one of the nuns was sent to a nearby house to ask to purchase it.

When she met the owner and went inside, she saw the most enormous accumulation of worthless stuff. Stacks of newspaper, debris, tons of furniture and dust. The clutter and filth was fairly shocking to the nun. The owner was a widow, very unpleasant and mean to the nun. She vowed she would never sell her house to the convent and was offended to be asked!

The nun left there feeling very critical of this woman for her shocking greed. But when she went to the Lord, she asked Him to show her this same sin in herself. In her barren living conditions she could have felt quite superior to this widow.

But the Lord showed her the one postcard she had kept. The rule of this Order was that you could own nothing, keep nothing for yourself. But in disobedience, the nun had kept that one postcard hidden away for herself. The Spirit of God struck her that in principle there was no difference between her and this unhappy woman. For both it was the slavery of greed.

The nun was broken and began to pray, "Lord, forgive US for OUR greed." She entered the sin with the widow and identified with her, confessing and asking forgiveness for them both.

In a short while, the widow called for the nun to return to her house. She gave the house freely to the convent.

Some of us carry such a load of guilt and sin that we are hopeless under that weight. The Lord gives His servants chances to extend forgiveness in all humility, confessing with *anyone* that we are equally as guilty.

Despite what Daniel suffered under Israel's captivity to Babylon, he is never seen as bitter or even resistant. He is always willing to serve his enemy faithfully and he survived through three kings, each of whom gave him honor and position.

The word forgive is mentioned only twice in Daniel's story. It was not about Daniel's forgiveness but rather his prayer for the forgiveness of God for Israel (Daniel 9:3-19).

After seeking God by prayer and fasting, Daniel confessed the sins of Israel this way: *"We have sinned, committed iniquity, acted wickedly and rebelled . . ."* Not *they*, but *we*.

Daniel even confessed that *"**we** have not earnestly begged for forgiveness and entreated the favor of the Lord our God, that we might turn from our iniquities"* (Daniel 9:13 AMPC).

If you are experienced in repentance, you know that whatever anyone else has done, you could have done the same given the right circumstance. And deeper still, you know that you *have done* the same, even if only in thought.

Forgiveness is a world-shaking power. To confess and forgive changes history, lifting the unbearable load of sin from others. The tragedy of humanity is sin and that has been solved to the uttermost.

Behold! the Lamb of God
who takes away the sin of the world.

As fully-forgiven-sinners, we are to be instruments of
God's unending mercy and dynamic grace, shaking the
world with the unknown freedom of forgiveness. We
hold in our own hands the power to set others free, by
knowing the radical and terrible price Jesus Christ paid
to extend forgiveness . . . to me, to you, and to the world.
We are the pivot of life or death by the mere act of choice:
"Forgive us our debts, as we also have forgiven our debtors"
(Matthew 6:12).

The principal of identifying in prayer is entering the
prison-of-sin with the sinner and rescuing them by the
faith of your own repentance and personal confession.
The Holy Spirit will bring this prayer, as we are willing to
be vessels of His intercession for prisoners and the Lost.

SETTING THE CAPTIVES FREE

You know firsthand the loving forgiveness of God's
merciful pardon. And you can cause the lost to know that
mercy also, just by confessing your sin that is like theirs.

God has never failed to show me my own likeness of
sin with someone who is cruel. No matter how awful
the sin, and how little I see how I can relate, God always
will point to the 'principle of the sin' and show me that I
am – at the base of my being – capable of doing or being
anything that any other human being is.

Jesus declared the *"release to the captives . . . to set free those who are oppressed"* (Luke 4:18). Sin is captivity and forgiveness is the release. We have the privilege of being ourselves released and extending God's mercy by vicarious prayer with the sinner. We enter their prison, by humility of identification, by confession, and receiving fresh forgiveness. Then we break open the prison door and set them free.

The end of Daniel's prayer was the appearance of Gabriel, the great angel, who comes and assures the man with a prophecy: *"To make an end of sin, to make atonement for iniquity, to bring everlasting righteousness . . ."*
And that was the promise of Christ's atonement for the sins Daniel had taken on himself.

JESUS ENTERED OUR BOX

This is the very thing Jesus did for mankind. He came down from a throne of glory, walked in the dust of common human life, and even put on the garb of a human body. He confined Himself to the lowest limitations of our unremarkable lives. He had one thing that made Him different, and that made ALL the difference. Jesus had God indwelling to live His life, think His thoughts, and SAY His words.

Instead of Jesus living in His humanity, there was the Father, living within the Son and always being the Life.

He experienced every temptation. He felt every possible response, 'yet without sin.' And He came to give us all freedom, all liberty . . .

Isaiah's prophecy about Christ was this:

He has sent Me to bind up the brokenhearted,
To proclaim liberty to the captives,
And freedom to the prisoners;
Isaiah 61:1b NASB

ENTERING THE PRISON

Let me tell you about the first evil person I ever knew.
I was a young woman and she was much older than me.
She was close in and I couldn't escape her.

Her 'words were softer than oil, yet they were drawn
swords' (Ps. 55:21 KJV).

On the one hand she praised me and on the other, she
shredded me with cruelty. I was utterly bewildered
by this. I had never met anyone like her and I had no
wisdom to understand it. I began to have nightmares
about her that left me puzzled. My dreams were trying
to tell me the reality: she really was murderous toward
me, with vicious intentions that were not evident in her
outward behavior.

One day I sat on a swing in my yard seeking the Lord
about her. I was defenseless and bewildered. And I
was shredded in my soul with a despair I had never
experienced. She claimed love and admiration, but what I
felt was extreme hatred.

I heard the Lord say, "She is evil."

I said, "Oh no, Lord, she talks about God.
                         She can't be *evil*."

In time, I knew He was right . . .

She was not merely a mean woman. She was truly evil.
She created discord, division, despair, and darkness in
everyone's life. Yet outsiders would never guess.

I had never met someone who was truly evil yet wore the
believable disguise of a 'good Christian' woman.

I tried to appease her, please her, escape her, and show
her the truth. Finally, I was assigned to take care of her,
which I did not resist, knowing it was God's will. But she
hated me the more because she needed me.

I tried to love her out of her hate for me. For years I
sought to solve her by something I could do or be. And
nothing worked. Nothing helped.

During it all I was walking with Christ and growing
in His love and His will. How she hated that! If I said I
couldn't eat supper because I was fasting, she hounded
me to eat, threatening that I would become sick. I hid
my Bible reading from her, I tried not to fast when eating
with her.

But my walk with Christ was becoming more visible. Her
religious façade increased and she became even more
cruel.

Finally I began to cry out to God.

I felt like the people in Egypt under cruel slavery. And God had been waiting for my endurance to come to an end so that I needed only Him, Who alone could help me and perhaps help her!

I began to live in Psalm 37. This Psalm of David set out exactly God's will for such a situation as he had with Saul, who was devoured by his jealousy of the favored David and tried to kill him at least 13 times. I outlined that Psalm, I prayed it, I tried to obey it.

Delight yourself in the Lord;
And He will give you the desires of your heart.
Commit your way to the Lord, Trust also in Him,
and He will do it.
Do not fret because of him who prospers in his way,
Because of the man who carries out wicked schemes.
Psalm 37:4-5, 7b NASB

It seemed to me that this woman was stronger than God. No one could affect her and no one could stop her.

My nemesis began to call *my* friends, telling them lies about me. I didn't know it for some time until one loyal friend told me about it. One friend told the woman she would not listen and not to ever call her again. She told her that she would not be part of her campaign of slander.

Another friend did listen, and by some chance remark I made, saw the truth. That friend said, "Oh Martha, she is lying about you!" She had obviously been persuaded! And she had not told me about the calls.

On and on it went, ever present – in my face – was her evil.

ALIKE!

I asked my Master to show me the same evil in me as was in her. And to my surprise, He did! I saw that I could hate her as much as she hated me. We were no different in possibility and in nature.

I had no idea I was capable of such hate! I had to confess to God and be forgiven for hating her. And I prayed deeply to know His love for her.

CHOSEN EVIL

I had come to understand how she stayed in her evil. She deliberately chose to be cruel and wicked. I watched her make clear choices to torment her family and her world. She continued to choose the meanest way with full understanding.

The choice was clear to her. For so long I believed her to be simply blind to herself, but I realized with shock that she knew exactly what she was doing and chose evil at every occasion! Also she admitted being well aware that God was confronting her, but she would not yield.

DEEP DESPAIR

Then in the middle of one agonizing night, I was weeping and crying out to the Lord. I said, "Lord, solve one of us. Take me home, or take her home!"
My despair was that deep.

That night the Lord said something to me so startling. He said, "I, God, have accepted her choice.
                           Who are you?"

I got it! His gift of free will is absolute. I was playing God, endlessly trying to get her to change her choices, to turn her will – for my sake! I was failing to change her and I was personally being destroyed. At that moment, I saw I was the one in the wrong. It was futile to fight her, to try to be good enough for her. God had let her have her way, and I was to join Him as Lord of all and give up trying to change her.

I was free from that time on. I was in God's good will for me and I was no longer striving with her will. I could take care of her needs gladly and I was immune to her demands and cruelty. I just went joyfully on my way, unaffected.

Strangely, when I stopped resisting her, she quit attacking me. Since it now had no affect, she gave up. One must end a fight of two. I had thought it should be her, but God meant it to be me.

Oswald Chambers said, "When you are insulted, you must make it an occasion to exhibit the Son of God. You cannot imitate the disposition of Jesus; it is either there or it is not."

Finally, by surrender to the Lord, Christ-in-me could obey that impossible command: *"Resist not the evil men do to you."* Christ Himself is the only One who can live in such abandon of trust in the Father. The old humanity can only resist. It is our nature to cry, "Injustice!"

By failure, I died to the flesh in the arena of nonresistance. And when I was freed, it was myself from whom I was liberated.

BREAKING THE CHAINS

I spent the next years praying fervently for her salvation. No matter what she was or what she had done, I couldn't bear that she might go to hell. I wasn't assured of her salvation so I no longer prayed for her to change or be nice for my sake. I begged God to bring her to salvation. Whatever I had suffered at her hand was nothing compared to that prospect of hell.

At the end of her life, she was hospitalized and I was with her every day. The doctors felt she would not live long.

One day when I walked in, she threw her arms open toward me and said, "Oh, I have been waiting for you! I have to change my life."

I had never heard such language from her before. I realized it was a critical moment. She was facing God in His final grace of repentance. I prayed silently and desperately, "Lord, what shall I do, what should I say?"

It came to me to say to her, "Will you forgive me for all the ways I have failed you?" She said a rather desperate "YES!"

Then she repeated my own words, addressed to me, "Will you forgive me for all the ways I have failed you?" I said, "Yes."

I went on to tell her about the cross, asking her to give her sins to the Lord Jesus, leave them on the cross, and let Him have it all. I don't remember all I said, but at the end she said, "I will, I will!"

She died a few days later, but there was a peace and quiet in her that had never been there before.

When she was about to face God, it was me she wanted and needed. And I was given at last the privilege to help her. Only through first, a radical surrender to God, and second, giving up my own fight. Then came forgiveness, love and . . . praise God, heaven came down!

IN THE BOX

My Sovereign Lord had long before asked me to lay down my life for this woman. Such was His integrity to give me the choice. And I did say yes to Him, though with dread.

And so He put me inside the terrible prison of her hate and rebellion. He asked me to break us both out of her chains. It took years of suffering and doing it the wrong way, but in the end of the story, God won over us both and it was worth it all.

I felt I had a college education in the subject of deliberate evil and the great mercy of God to save even the worst of us. I also have the very sober sense that if I had not changed myself and instead continued fighting her choice, she might be in hell for eternity. And who knows where I would be – certainly a bitter, failing woman!

The privilege of this long, terrible experience is one of my best gifts from God. I know the lengths He will go to save a wretched soul, so precious to Him, and with no deserving of it! I love Him for that merciful forgiveness, for me as well.

And I love Him for Who He is to me, that He would purge *me of evil* as He was pursuing her. His ways are brilliant and holy, His ending of the story, *if we let Him write it,* is perfect.

It was through this enemy and from My Lord that I learned how to forgive and how to overcome evil with good by HIS love for my enemy, operating through me.

I had to be forgiven of my own arrogance and hate first. Then I could overcome that of my enemy and lead her to Christ.

I was a prisoner of her evil for decades. God put me there by HIS immovable choice and asked me to agree to His will. The Sovereign Lord had in mind a purpose so great, so glorious for me, that had I understood in the beginning, I would have gladly volunteered for that terrible Box.

Above all the many lessons, the wonderful principles I learned, the most important thing was coming to know a little more about God's heart, His ways, and His unfathomable Love.

I discovered an amazing thing:
the Father is so quietly at work deep within the spirit,
                    ever conforming us to the image of His Son.

Our cries are heard.
Our needs are met.

And one bright day we discover that
the transforming power of God
was intimately with us all along the Way.

*And God is able to **make all grace** abound to you,
so that always having **all sufficiency** in everything,
you may have an abundance for every good deed;
2 Corinthians 9:8 NASB (emphasis mine)*

Humility Is...

Humility is . . . freedom from your own driven ego.

Humility is . . . knowing you yourself desperately require forgiveness as the greatest of all needs.

Humility is . . . being little, being NOTHING.

Being nothing is having nothing to defend, to explain, to achieve. No place, no acclaim, no vindication, no praise, no notice, no . . . anything.

When you are nothing, you need nothing.

Without the brokenness that produces deep humility,
true forgiveness is impossible . . .
and will never happen.

Wrapped in Christ's acceptance and lost in His love,
you need nothing else on this earth, from this world.

Humility is . . . loving heaven's reward more than earth's acclaim, living only for God's defense and the inevitable justice of that Last Day.

And yet, humility is . . . knowing what you really deserve and, out of that constant awareness, freeing all others who deserve the same as you.

Humility is . . . the bedrock of forgiveness.
Humility *will forgive!*

Humility is . . . surrender to need-and-nothingness as a way of life.

Humility is . . . a common empty vessel, ever content to wait for the water of the Spirit.

Only the deepest humility will let the Blood of Christ be enough for mountains of wrong.

Living in Grace

The new creation lives immersed in God's forgiveness. That is GRACE. It is a state of being, not a place to visit when in desperation. The new man is possessed by the new nature of Christ Himself. So the 'new self' lives above offenses – they are irrelevant and have no power. To the new creation, forgiveness is a finished gift, so lavish that you simply receive in a constant flow of the Blood of the Beloved. You . . . let.

The 'new creation' is not an ideal. It is at last, the Real. There is not a 'must do' but an 'already finished' by which we live. There is no try, no strive, for all is done.

**Grace is the power of God *within us*
to live His character . . . His very Life.**

Therefore, let us fear if, while a promise remains of entering His rest, any one of you may seem to have come short of it.
Hebrews 4:1 NASB

Because all the problem of humanity is carried away and then recreated anew and borne for us, we can rest.

Our sin is dealt with by the old man's grave with Christ. Our problem of living is solved.
Now we are possessed by a Life that pleases God, without Law, without effort.

It is all finished. We can rest in that which is done FOR us, IN us, without us.

Is this hard to understand?
Does it sound too good?
Is it unbelievable?

Of course! We have rarely known this. And God must reveal it from heaven.

> *. . . those who receive the abundance of grace*
> *and of the gift of righteousness*
> *will reign in life through the One, Jesus Christ.*
> *Romans 5:17b NASB*

As you stumble along, you will need grace,
and when you need it, God will reveal it.

> *But to the one who does not work, but believes on Him*
> *who declares the ungodly to be righteous,*
> *his faith is credited for righteousness.*
> *Romans 4:5 HCSB*

Forgiveness and Healing

It is clear and real that Jesus' suffering and forgiveness
solved every human problem,
including the terrible problem of illness.

But [in fact] He has borne our griefs,
And He has carried our sorrows and pains . . .

But He was wounded for our transgressions,
He was crushed for our wickedness
[our sin, our injustice, our wrongdoing];
The punishment [required] for our well-being fell on Him,
And by His stripes (wounds) we are healed.
Isaiah 53:4a, 5 AMP (emphasis mine)

The word sorrows actually means 'sickness.'
So twice it is written that He took into Himself and
carried . . . our sicknesses and our punishment for sins.

In the New Covenant, the first requirement for healing is
the confession of sin. Sin is the one barrier to God's real
gift of healing by the Cross of Jesus.

Since sin is fully forgiven,
it is easy to remove the barrier of sin,
either by forgiving or being forgiven.

Is anyone among you sick?
He should call for the elders of the church,
and they should pray over him after anointing him
with olive oil in the name of the Lord.
The prayer of faith will save the sick person,
and the Lord will restore him to health;
if he has committed sins, he will be forgiven.

> *Therefore, confess your sins to one another and*
> *pray for one another, so that you may be healed.*
> *The urgent request of a righteous person*
> *is very powerful in its effect.*
> James 5:14-16 HCSB

The *Holman Christian Standard* version is a very accurate translation. The first action in sickness is to seek the Lord for the Holy Spirit to reveal sin in your life. There is power and promise in confessing to those you trust and to your 'spiritual guides' (*Amplified Bible*). Dealing with sin is either seeking forgiveness or giving forgiveness.

I am not legalistic about this passage in James. For those who aren't healed, I don't judge. God alone knows why and for what purpose, and He is the Keeper of our days.

REFUSING CONFESSION

I know someone who was seriously ill. This person was given the following gracious word from the Lord.

> *Do not be wise in your own eyes;*
> *Fear the Lord and turn away from evil.*
> *It will be healing to your body*
> *And refreshment to your bones.*
> Proverbs 3:7-8 NASB

Diagnosis: arrogance, no fear of God,
and living in evil.
Remedy: to cultivate humility and fear of God,
and leave your evil ways.
Result: the promise of healing and health.

But this person refused to repent and confess . . . and in a short time, died.

The whole issue of forgiving is a life and death matter.

FAITH TO PRAY

Faith of the ones who pray is the other requirement for healing. When we pray for the sick,
the Lord gives Christ's own faith for healing.

"The prayer of faith will save the sick person . . ."

A LIVING EXPERIENCE

Here is one of my personal experiences with healing.

Several years ago, I was speaking in Slovakia and Austria when I became very sick. Even when I returned home, I remained ill for many weeks. I was given a strong antibiotic but it had no effect.

Finally I was stricken with excruciating pain and taken to the emergency room at the hospital. Many tests filled that first day, and at last I was told there was a 'soft tissue mass' in my small intestine. Surgeons would see me the next morning to arrange for immediate surgery.

I understood that this was very serious, perhaps cancer.

During the night I told the Lord that if He wanted to take me home, I was willing; it was His choice. If He chose to raise me up, it was only to serve Him and not for any other reason.

Then I heard Him clearly:
> "There is no blood on your hands.
> I cannot withhold healing from you."

I turned over and went to sleep.

The next morning there were more x-rays. When the two surgeons came in, they said the tumor was gone and no surgery was planned. Overnight the tumor had vanished as I slept. I could hardly take it in, but I had two x-rays – one with a tumor and one with none!

It seems I was up to date with obedience, forgiving, and confessing. At that time, there was no barrier of sin between the Lord and me, and I was healed.

On another occasion, I was praying for my husband, who was suffering from a terrible rare disease. I was praying fervently when suddenly the Holy Spirit came into the prayer with boldness beyond my capacity. And I began to cry out with a loud voice to God,

> "You KNOW he is forgiven. You have to heal him!"

I sensed the Lord's pleasure and I heard this word, "Done."

The healing was evident when symptoms disappeared, and even the doctor said it was a miracle.

The Holy Spirit is the origin and power of prayer.

He intercedes for the saints according to the will of God.
Romans 8:26-28 NLT

Emphasizing persistent prayer, Jesus gave this parable of the *Friend at Midnight*:

I tell you, even though he will not get up and give him anything
just because he is his friend,
yet because of his persistence and boldness
he will get up and give him whatever he needs.
Luke 11:8 AMP

By my own experiences and by faith in the scriptures, I do believe healing is as much a part of the atonement as forgiveness of sin.

Therefore repent and return,
so that your sins may be wiped away,
in order that times of refreshing may come
from the presence of the Lord,
and that He may send Jesus,
the Christ appointed for you.
Acts 3:19-20 NASB

The Mystery of the Cross

Incarnation.
Crucifixion.
Resurrection.
Ascension.
Pentecost.

The Life of One who came down to us
also took us up in Him to heaven!

Seeking the Cross

Even as a small child in Methodist Sunday School, the cross was a strange mystery to me. "Why did the sweet Jesus have to die *for me?*" I felt I wasn't that much of a sinner and that He didn't need to have died for me. I grieved that He died on the cross but I couldn't understand why He had to.

I didn't want Him to suffer and die and I would say to Him, "Why did you die for me? I never asked you to do that. I'm so sorry you suffered and died."

I left it at that for some years, an unsolved mystery. It was too big for me. And I was right. The Cross looms so large in time and space that its significance and power are lost even on those of us who have been saved because of it.

When I came to repentance in my twenties,
           I saw sin in wrenching clarity.

God revealed His Son and I was covered by grace.
        And the Cross became dear . . .
              but still not fully understood.

THE CROSS IS POWER

> *But we who are being saved know*
> *it is the very power of God.*
> *1 Corinthians 1:18b NLT*

The Cross is the *"very power of God"*?

Then we need to see the Cross in all its meaning,
by its vast power and unfathomable impact.
For without help from God,
without the revelation of the Holy Spirit,
the Cross remains the symbol over the altar.
A sentimental emblem we wear.

We know the doctrine but we are far from the reality of this great Dark Tree that invades the long story of humanity.

The Cross that divided Time and History,
is the end of the Terrible-Old
and the beginning of the Amazing-New.
All of which is so stunning, so perfect that
the natural mind cannot see it,
much less understand it.

The most brilliant intellect could never imagine
the power that Jesus released
through the Cross.

THE FOOLISHNESS OF THE CROSS

We are at the mercy of God who longs to reveal this 'foolish' thing of the cross. We are stunned that God would kill His own Son for love of the world.

For the message of the cross is foolishness
to those who are perishing,
but to us who are being saved it is the power of God.
1 Corinthians 1:18 NKJV

Why a cross? Who knows what it all means?

Yes, Jesus died to pay for our sins. Yes, to bear our
punishment. This we think we know and we settle for
that – it is phenomenal enough. I am satisfied.

But my needs are critical in this journey through life.

My needs are not yet met and I seem to know that
the Cross of Christ is my entire answer and my future.

Through His own flesh, Christ rent the veil that separates
us from God. *"It is finished"* . . . yet I find the Cross is my
own life and death.

The Cross of Christ is living.
The Cross pursues me. It wants something of me.
The Cross crosses my path as a very persistent Reality.

> Life in all its crises demands that
> I know more about that
> strange and solemn Crossed Tree.

Truly! What did Jesus finish?

The Lamb took away the sin of the world. That's all we
know. Jesus swallowed death and carried away sin, but
He also *gave* . . .

The great and vast treasure
poured on us from the Cross—
this we do not see or receive,
even though the Bible clearly names it.

BEHOLD THE CROSS

God's Son was dying at noon.
>For the three hours of His dying,
>blackest day fell on the whole world of murderers.

>>*Now from the sixth hour darkness fell*
>>*upon all the land until the ninth hour.*
>>*Matthew 27:45 NASB*

Jesus' loud cry was His final voice.
The veil separating us from God was torn in two from
top to bottom. And the way to the Secret Holiest Place
was opened to all.

>>*And Jesus uttered a loud cry, and breathed His last.*
>*And the veil of the temple was torn in two from top to bottom.*
>>*Mark 15:37-38 NASB*

By the bloody shredding of Jesus' body,
the separation of His joints and the piercing of the spear,
>His body became the very door,
>hideously split open for our access to God . . .
>>**where He is!**

>>*Therefore, brethren, since we have confidence*
>>*to enter the holy place by the blood of Jesus,*
>*by a new and living way which He inaugurated for us*
>>***through the veil, that is, His flesh.***
>>*Hebrews 10:19-20 NASB*

By One holy death, Life was released.
>That Life struck the dead awake by its power.

The earth shook, rocks split apart and tombs opened.
The bodies of many godly men and women
who had died were raised from the dead.
Matthew 27:51b-52 NLT

When Jesus died, the earth of His creation mourned
and heaved for Him, and terror fell on the watchers,
to behold His Sonship at last.

Now the centurion, and those who were with Him
keeping guard over Jesus,
when they saw the earthquake
and the things that were happening
became very frightened and said,
"Truly this was the Son of God!"
Matthew 27:54 NASB

SOMETHING BIG IS FINISHED

Therefore when Jesus had received the sour wine,
He said, "It is finished!"
And He bowed His head
and gave up His spirit.
John 19:30 NASB

That strange final statement of Christ: *It is finished!*

It meant more than His suffering was over.
In my spirit, I knew that statement reached across the
universe and completed something so vast I couldn't see
its infinity.

The Finish was brought to its "perfect end and its destined goal" (Strong's G5055).

If this is my answer, and it declares that something is utterly and finally finished, my heart's need is desperate to know – *what was finished?*

I read the commentary: "The whole work of salvation was finished."

But that merely raises again the question:
What IS the whole work of salvation?
Tell me, Lord.

Uunfixable Humanity

God has a beginning of all things but He also has a finish. Everything He originates will have its perfect fulfillment, its flawless completion. God being perfect, makes all things perfect. Only perfection will satisfy God.

God finished creation on the sixth day and declared it complete to His own satisfaction.

He created humanity on the sixth day and gave Adam and Eve two gifts: free will and dominion of the earth. Immediately the woman and the man used their free will to reject God and surrender their rule over the world to His enemy! So humanity was corrupted and their dominion lost.

*The Lord saw that the wickedness of man was great in the earth, and that **every intention of the thoughts of his heart was only evil continually.***
*And the Lord regretted that he had made man on the earth, and **it grieved him to his heart**.*

So the Lord said, "I will blot out man whom I have created from the face of the land, man and animals and creeping things and birds of the heavens, for I am sorry that I have made them." But Noah found favor in the eyes of the Lord.
Genesis 6:5-13 ESV (emphasis mine)

The Lord brought the great flood of 40 days, and every living thing drowned except what was in the ark with Noah.

The Father wanted to begin a new race of humanity descending from Noah, the one righteous man who 'walked with God.' But Noah was still afflicted with the corruption he had inherited from Adam and Eve. Humanity's immorality had not drowned in the flood.

In a short time, Noah was found drunk from his own wine, exposing his naked shame before his sons.

And humanity went downhill once more, not able to last even with the goodness of the only favored man, who ended in shame and degradation.

Humanity was corrupted by inheritance.

A NEW NATION

Next, the LORD built a new nation beginning with Abram. This He said to Abram:
> *"Walk before me and be perfect"* (Gen. 17:1).

He gave everything to this new nation, including the blood sacrifice to pay for sin. He also brought His constantly available presence into the tabernacle. God withheld nothing from this nation, giving them everything they wanted, including a king.

But Israel worshiped other gods, refused to hear Him and would not - because they could not - obey His laws. Israel also fell downward into rebellion and disobedience, and turned a hard heart to God.

God tried to remake humanity twice.
By His patient forbearing, He proved that the original
humanity was hopeless and impossible of change.

The human race was utterly and hopelessly depraved.

> *All have turned away; all alike have become corrupt.*
> *There is no one who does good,*
> *not even one.*
> *Psalm 53:3 HCSB*

We must remember . . .
    God being perfect, requires perfection.

Despite His goodness and patience,
        His giving and forgiving,
        His vast provision and His faithful love,
            humanity could not be changed.

**There was not one perfectly good person,
century upon century!**

The Perfect Man

To perfect His creation of mankind,
God needed a perfect man
and there was . . . *'not one.'*

The One Perfect Being was God's *only* begotten Son,
but He was God and not man! And the problem was a
malignant humanity, void of any uprightness.

In the councils of the Most High, the Father asked the Son
to leave His glory, His seat in the heavenly throne and
enter the terrible race of depraved humanity,
as a common,
even poor and unremarkable,
Perfect Man.

So Christ was born, as all are, by a mother into a human
body. But the secret of His uncommon life was this:
His real father was THE real Father.

This Perfect Man was the only good Man who had ever
lived. It was from Adam, that one original man, that
all humanity descended and all were born corrupted,
without hope of change. That Adamic nature we have
all inherited.

The Perfect Man was humanly alive,
but He had not come to live.
He had come to *die!*

He came to drink the cup of God's wrath against all
humankind. He was sent to receive the punishment
due to all who had lived and ever would live.

He swallowed the death that every person earned by his
or her imperfect morality.

> Jesus, the Last Adam,
>> brought a final end to human wickedness.

Our prison door is open now,
> and our Redeemer waits to give us . . .
>> His Perfect Self.

What Did the Cross Finish?

Sin was paid for. Death was conquered. Grief was borne.
That is the clean up of human mess and demise.
This is all we have known about the Cross.

But for me a huge Mystery remained.
Something so much more was accomplished and I knew
the strange "It is finished" was bigger than human mind
could imagine. I asked and prayed to see . . . "What was it
YOU finished?"

Jesus said this as His last word: "It is finished."
　　　　　He also cried out in saying it.
　　　　　Was it a cry of agony or release?
Then He bowed His head and surrendered His soul
voluntarily to God – and He died.

I wondered deeply, "WHAT was finished?"
　　　　It was the big question left unanswered,
　　　　even after many priceless answers were given.

I spent a morning with the Lord asking to know the
answer. And suddenly I understood . . .

THIS is finished! Our entire human nature, the one that
failed the Father, rejected the Spirit, and killed Jesus. It
was a problem of the very nature of mankind.

Now the human nature that did only what was wrong,
and could not change, died with Christ. The whole race
of fallen mankind went into the grave with Him. A literal
race of mankind, dead and buried with Jesus.

For we know that our old self was crucified with Him
in order that sin's dominion over the body may be abolished,
so that we may no longer be enslaved to sin,
Romans 6:6 HCSB

We humans are a species with a set of characteristics and shared values: a self-worshiping, I-am-god identity. Jesus took that old self into Himself and died with it!

An entire fallen race consisting of every person of any ethnicity and from every culture, this is what died with Christ – IN Christ. This vast humanity full of good-and-evil wickedness, He joined Himself to us. Then He died with all humanity from Eden to the end of time.

He put an end to our soul-sick nature,
       that couldn't be fixed or drowned or supported.

Jesus joined our frail humanity. Born of a human, He lived in our flesh and blood condition; He entered the box of our imprisoned condition and broke us out as innocent beings.

              He took both our sin and our disposition
                     to the grave of a permanent death.

The One Perfect Man, died for an imperfect humanity, hopeless and helpless. To forgive us would have been an amazing gift, but it was more than forgiveness. It was to remove the very source of sin, the 'old man.'

       He died *for us.*
              He died *with us.*
                     And our sin nature died *with Him.*

All fallen humanity – born dead and hopeless –
in Christ is fallen . . . away!

RAISED TO THE NEW

There was another 'finish!' Jesus rose from the grave by
a power so dynamic that it has been likened to an atomic
blast.

Jesus, raised from death, brought to life in Himself a new
breed of humanity, a God-filled and Christ-like *nature*.
An immortal being, victorious and limitless.

Out of the grave, Jesus brought forth a new creation of
man and woman, not a conversion of the old. A new
creation brought forth from nothing of the old nature, an
entirely new being, utterly unlike its predecessor.

All Adamic characteristics died and now there remains
just one nature, Jesus Christ.

*And although you were formerly alienated and hostile in mind,
engaged in evil deeds, yet He has now reconciled you*
***in His fleshly body through death, in order to present
you***
before Him holy and blameless and beyond reproach . . .
Colossians 1:21-22 NASB (emphasis mine)

Humanity reborn is created *all new*. It is literally a new
race of men, bearing a likeness to the Perfect Man,
possessing a capability never before present in any
person: the ability to live like Jesus, by having His very
nature.

What was finished? At last, humanity is finished,
perfectly aligned to God's original idea of many sons
like His One Son.

**Jesus revived God's original dream
for His lost children.**

What the first Adam ruined, the Last Adam restored.

*And just as Christ was raised from the dead
by the glorious power of the Father,
now we also may live new lives.*
Romans 6:4b NLT

Born again to a living hope. You must be born again.

Now there is no problem but one:
     to *believe* this outlandish solution,
     to pray, to read, to ponder . . .
     and above all, *bow* –
          until this strange, unfathomable
          accomplishment of God is exploded into
          a reality that is practical and accessible!

*For neither is circumcision anything [of any importance],
nor uncircumcision, but [only] a new creation
[which is the result of a new birth—a spiritual transformation—
a new nature in Christ Jesus].*
Galatians 6:16 AMP (emphasis mine)

But far be it from me to glory
[in anything or anyone] except
in the cross of our Lord Jesus Christ
(the Messiah) through Whom
the world has been crucified to me,
and I to the world!
Galatians 6:14 AMP

It Is Finished

It is finished.
Salvation added to forgiveness,
  grace above reconciliation.
    A gift beyond redemption . . . a new self.

Divine Abiding

For those who are born again,
there is an entirely new life within,
the very life of Christ.

Living becomes a process of discovering Jesus,
beyond, within, and everywhere.

God's plan, realized in Christ, is too fantastic to grasp.
His wonders of Eternal Life, only a child could believe.

Where I am, He is.

Dwell in Me, and I will dwell in you.
[Live in Me, and I will live in you.]
John 15:4 AMPC

I am hiding there in Him.

[For] your old sinful self has . . . died, and
your new life is kept [hidden] with Christ in God.
Colossians 3:3 EXB

Where He is, I am.

For he raised us from the dead along with Christ
and seated us with him in the heavenly realms
because we are united with Christ Jesus.
Ephesians 2:6 NLT

I will forever be with Him.

Everyone who lives and believes in Me
will never die—ever. Do you believe this?
John 11:26 HCSB

The Startling Little Word

I read it all, every book in the Bible.
More than reading, I loved it, soaked in it, drank it.
All the holy Words the Spirit wrote
    were precious to my heart, amazing to my mind.
      But I missed the one word that hid
        and contained the meaning of it All.

Once I saw that tiny insignificant word,
I found its placement everywhere.

      The mighty word is . . . **IN.**

      *Abide **in** Me and I **in** you.*

      *Whoever abides **in** Me and I **in** him,*
        he it is that bears much fruit . . .
      John 15:4a, 5b ESV (emphasis mine)

      He who eats My flesh and drinks My blood
        *abides **in** Me, and I **in** him*
      John 6:56 NASB (emphasis mine)

The Greek meaning of the little **IN:**
    "A marker of close personal association
    IN, one with, in union with, joined closely to."[1]

      God is not only WITH me.
        Christ is not merely FOR me.
          He is **IN** me.

This is the oneness for which Jesus prayed so fervently in
His final prayer.

There can be no greater intimacy than to be indwelt.
God has removed my sinful separation and made us
ONE! I cannot seek Him as apart from me. I seek Him
only to have this oneness manifest, to be experienced.
My only need is to believe that startling word – **IN**.

I long for intimacy with God
>   but He has sought intimacy with ME
>   and made it possible at His own great expense!

He has broken every barrier down. Amazing Grace!

I do not ask on behalf of these alone,
but for those also who believe in Me through their word;
that they may all be one; even as You,
*Father, are **in** Me and I **in** You, that they also may be **in** Us.*
John 17:20-21a NASB (emphasis mine)

---

[1] Louw-Nida 89:119

Another Life Lives

I have been crucified with Christ
[in Him I have shared His crucifixion];
it is no longer I who live, but
Christ (the Messiah) lives in me;
and the life I now live in the body I live by faith in
(by adherence to and reliance on and complete trust in)
the Son of God, Who loved me
and gave Himself up for me.
Galatians 2:20 AMPC

This one verse is the answer to our every need—
Not I, but Christ.
Christ lives in me.

Every command and every principle of scripture has
a secret. And for every question and every need – and
indeed every command of Scripture – the answer is
always Christ. Simply Christ.

Every command of the New Testament is addressed to
Christ in YOU, the new man, and not you, the old self.
The 'old man' cannot live such high and holy things.

Christ IS the treasure; His Life is the power and His Life
in all its fullness dwells IN me.
And this is the one solution.

Christ within is my personal fountain of forgiveness.

To depend on God within—this is how Jesus lived and
how we are to live. By another life, another creation,
another capacity.

Jesus lived entirely by Another's thoughts,
    Another's purity,
    Another's very energy.

Leave the old man and all God-Life
    will flow in you, from you.

There is grace equal to every offense. Grace, the strength
of God imparted to the weakness of humanity . . . from
within.

There is Only One capable of complete forgiveness.
        One Alone is the source and spring of forgiveness
            and we must drink of Jesus' Life whose
                forgiveness is a gift—No!
                    Even more . . . a miracle.

Sin, the unbearable burden, was nailed to the Cross, laid
on Him who had no sin. The human heart in its total
"inclination toward evil" has no capacity for forgiving to
the uttermost.

Dear Lord Jesus,

Even my faithfulness must come from You,
every character quality must be YOU.
        YOU are integrity.
            YOU are forgiveness.
                You are. I am not.

**The way is a Person and the power is the Law of the
Spirit.**

His is the Life in me that *Lives me* instead of me.
And that living Life is the Resurrection life of Christ.
Christ, the Person of God, who is all I must be.

Jesus is the whole, the entire. He forgave all and He
forgives in and through me.

The heart of Jesus, who knows all . . . forgives all.
And the matchless power of His gracious forgiveness is
mine.

The blank truth about us dusty humans is this:
  I must forgive but I cannot forgive.

Spoken by Joseph, that man who suffered unspeakable
injustice:

> *"God has made me forget*
> *all my trouble and all my father's household."*

> *"God has made me fruitful*
> *in the land of my affliction."*
> *Genesis 41:51, 52 NASB*

Joseph declared what God had done for him, not what he
conquered on his own. God Himself had solved it all in
the deepest core of the man's heart.

Joseph was made to forget his suffering and more, to bear
fruit in the very land of his many afflictions. This can be
your story and your testimony.

God levels me in the wilderness so I find my helplessness.
Then He can be ALL He wants to be in my troubling
situation.

God must work inside me
    His own Acceptance and Divine Forgiveness
        for the enemies of my soul.

To receive it waits only for me to desperately need it.

We are looking for ease.
God is after emptiness . . .
that His Son might be our triumphant fullness.

Jesus' Great Assignments

Jesus clearly knew His God-given purpose on earth.
Such an enormous assignment we cannot imagine!
And all of it was for our redemption and salvation.

Jesus finished it all for you.
He gave His all for our all.

Jesus knew when His tasks were completed and then He
surrendered His spirit to God. Ever aware of the Father's
ultimate goal, He spoke often of the work given to Him to
accomplish. Oh, such works!

Jesus finished His life's purpose in every part.

- Matthew 5:17   to fulfill the law and the Prophets
- Matthew 20:28   to give His life a ransom for many

- Luke 4:43   to preach the good news
- Luke 12:49   to bring division into the family
- Luke 19:10   to seek and save the lost

- John 3:15   to give eternal life
- John 3:17   to save the world
- John 4:34   to finish His (God's) work

- John 9:39   to bring judgment – that those who are blind may see and those who see may become blind

- John 10:10   they may have life and have it abundantly

- John 12:47   to save the world

- John 17:19   to sanctify Himself so that we may also be sanctified

- John 18:37   to be King – for this purpose I was born

- Romans 5:6   to die for the ungodly

- Galatians 1:4   to give Himself for our sins; to rescue us from the present evil age

- 1 Timothy 1:15   to save sinners

- Titus 2:14   to redeem us from all wickedness and to purify for Himself a people that are His very own

- Revelation 1:5   to us from our sins by His blood

- Revelation 5:9   to purchase men for God from every tribe

These and many more were the works God gave His Son to finish. And so they were.

Jesus declared these works perfectly accomplished.

And His ultimate obedience
was the horrifying crucifixion
that secured all His sacrifices.

Jesus could say to His dear Father:

*I have glorified You on the earth
by completing the work You gave Me to do.
John 17:4 HCSB*

Jesus has accomplished all and given all.
And we have huge blessings
yet to see, believe, and receive!

God on the Throne

The Bible admits of no rival power to
the throne of the Most High God.

His Perfection in Suffering

There is a sovereign Hand behind all the bombardment of life.

God is in charge of your history and in control of your suffering. He creates an unfathomable purpose, an infinite good behind every offense, wrong, and injustice.

This is not a world of chaos and happenstance. The child of God lives under an order of the highest – and most mysterious – of all dominions.

God is on the throne and there is no rival to His power and no usurper of His chair.

> *. . . but all things are open and exposed,*
> *naked and defenseless*
> *to the eyes of Him with Whom we have to do.*
> *Hebrews 4:13b AMPC*

The entirety of this Christian life is to discover that God is truly God and there is no other.

It is God "with Whom we have to do!"
                                    Not humanity. Not Satan.

ALL MUST PASS THROUGH GOD

It is clear that Satan must ask permission
to touch the child of God.

Altogether Forgiven

Jesus said to Peter,

> *"Simon, Simon, behold, Satan has demanded permission*
> *to sift you like wheat; but I have prayed for you,*
> *that you faith may not fail and you,*
> *when once you have turned again, strengthen your brothers."*
> *Luke 22:31-32 NASB*

Permission demanded, permission granted. There was a sovereign purpose. It is clear. Peter's great claim to die for Jesus was sincere but self-deceived.

Satan had a season of permission, but his scheme failed. He wanted to shame and destroy Peter, but the man was kept by the prayer of Jesus. And so are you.

The Father let Peter be tossed around and betray Jesus to discover his own heart, and repent in the most painful regret. Then the man 'turned again' and Peter became a great apostle to the first century believers . . . and to us.

Simon Peter, the stone (actually a small pebble), was the kind of person on which Jesus would build His true church. Simon Peter, a man of reckless abandon, unvarnished adoration of the Lord . . . became one who would and *did die* in the utmost loyal love to his Lord. Crucified upside down, he considered himself unworthy to be crucified like Jesus.

This weak but passionate man, sifted for a brief time, was one of the closest disciples to Jesus.
Peter was with Him on the Mount of Transfiguration, and there at the Gethsemane arrest. He and John were the first disciples to run to the empty tomb.

Peter was the primary speaker at Pentecost, explaining the Holy Spirit and the scriptures to the thousands there.

FEEDING SHEEP TODAY

Peter 'turned again' as Jesus knew he would. He would go on to write two great themes in the scriptures.

The first theme (1 Peter), 'Victory over Suffering,' was written from his personal experience of continuous suffering and a profound understanding of Christ's suffering.

The second theme (2 Peter) is a warning of 'False Teachers and Apostasies of the Last Days.'

Simon Peter covered all the needs of this age,
    feeding lambs and tending Jesus' flock
    of believing sheep,
        for centuries, down to you and me.

He is the blessed and only Sovereign,
the King of kings, and the Lord of lords,
the only One who has immortality,
dwelling in unapproachable light;
no one has seen or can see Him,
to Him be honor and eternal might.
Amen.
1 Timothy 6:15b-16 HCSB (emphasis mine)

PAUL'S THORN IN THE FLESH

Paul was taken to Paradise, the third heaven.
He could not speak of it nor boast about it. It was too
sacred and too astounding. To keep the man humble after
such a vision, he was struck with a messenger of Satan
that actually was Paul's keeping and protection from his
own dangerous pride.

Paul was assigned to write most of the epistles in the
New Testament. The size of his suffering, chastening, and
torment was the size of his eternal significance . . . for you
and for me.

Because of the surpassing greatness of the revelations,
for this reason, to keep me from exalting myself,
there was given me a thorn in the flesh,
a messenger of Satan to torment me—
to keep me from exalting myself!
Concerning this I implored the Lord
three times that it might leave me.
And He has said to me, "My grace is sufficient for you,
for power is perfected in weakness." Most gladly, therefore, I
will rather boast about my weaknesses, so that the power of
Christ may dwell in me.

Therefore I am well content with weaknesses, with insults,
with distresses, with persecutions, with difficulties,
for Christ's sake; for when I am weak, then I am strong.
2 Corinthians 12:7-10 NASB (emphasis mine)

Our sufferings have a profound meaning in God's divine
protection and formation of our vesseled life. We dare
not define, categorize, or presume to know who, what, or
why.

God will always explain . . . in His flawless timing.
We ask, trust, and wait.

His control of all events and every disaster is perfect,
   that is obvious and clear from the whole Bible.

Nothing comes to us but through His governing Hand.
Satan's attack and human evil hide a Divine Purpose for
our destiny.

And we know [with great confidence] that God
[who is deeply concerned about us]
causes all things to work together [as a plan]
for good for those who love God,
to those who are called according to His plan and purpose.
Romans 8:28 AMP

Forgiveness is never finished until it turns to the
Only One with the Only power. The offense remains
smoldering underground, ready to erupt at any time.

We all know, with an inborn knowing,
   that God is the ultimate controller,
      so all offenses with life
         are ultimately directed at Him.

That which is known about God is evident within them;
for God made it evident to them.
For since the creation of the world
His invisible attributes, His eternal power and divine nature,
have been clearly seen, being understood through
what has been made so that they are without excuse.
Romans 1:19-20 NASB

The root of bitterness is at work in the darkness of
the soul, ever increasing in its sick contagion, all quite
unconsciously taking over ground that had previously
been cleansed by forgiveness. You can forgive and *still*
lose that forgiveness.

You can gain the grace to forgive the offender,
but until you know with certainty
that God is God,
forgiveness is not finished.

The Bible admits of no rival power
to the throne of the Most High.

There is purpose to all suffering,
and God is willing to reveal
His secrets about you, to you.
But it must be on the other side of bowing to Him as
the one and only God and Jesus Christ, His only Son.

Through the Son God made the whole universe,
and to the Son he has ordained that all creation
shall ultimately belong.

This Son, radiance of the glory of God,
flawless expression of the nature of God,
himself the upholding principle of all that is,
effected in person the reconciliation between God and man
and then took his seat at the right hand
of the majesty on high—thus proving himself,
by the more glorious name that he has won,
far greater than all the angels of God.
Hebrews 1:2-4 Phillips

Sovereign Offenses

Reading Hebrews 12:1-11

God is the Brooding Father to His children, knowing
all their weak spots and unexposed sickness. He is in
absolute control of what touches His growing children
and is the Blessed Controller of their experiences and . . .
enemies. I say again,

> We are after ease.
> > God is after emptiness . . .
> > > that His Son might be the fullness.

God is in relentless pursuit of the Old Man/Woman, to
hound them into the rightful grave of their hopelessness.

Father God is out to destroy in us the Old Man, and
resurrect – in us – the New Man. New Man being . . .

> *Christ in you, the hope of glory.*
> *Colossians 1:27*

God is intent on bringing children into the likeness of His
Cherished Son by the indwelling Life of Christ.

But we resist, in ignorance of the level of our depravity,
and by arrogance that insists on living for God according
to our own assessment.

> **So . . . the Cross of our solution brings to us
> personal wrongs by daily confrontation.**

God sends the proud to expose my preening pride, the evil to uncover my latent wickedness, the angry to spark my fire of rage.

Offenses that bombard me are a frightful mirror forcing me to see the face I have not known. And to ask forgiveness for attitudes that shock me, things my Father knew all along.

His scourging hand is behind every wound
and is a Lovely Father's perfect correction for a
secret Divine Purpose,
a Joseph-in-the-making
in me...

Offenses begin with family, the closest, most vulnerable ties . . . The wrongs extend to the workplace of Potiphar, where a miserable prison is the reward for fidelity.

But Joseph, in the brilliance of his comprehension, saw the Hand behind the many cruel hands of his history, truly every person of his journey.

Joseph bowed to that Divine Hand, who burned and chiseled the vessel of his soul into a Sterling Chalice, trusted with containing God in a foreign place of reigning.

**God chastens those He loves
with "scourging" like that which
He allowed His Son
to experience.**

With death blows to pride and wrestlings with Jacob-strength to break his "thigh."

For whom the Lord loves He chastens,
and scourges every son whom He receives.
Hebrews 12:6 NKJV

The offense is easier to accept if the Ruling Father is seen as Supremely Right and Sovereignly Loving in all He sends.

As with Joseph, forgiveness becomes
the crisis of my own destiny and
the very means to its discovery!

Forgiveness of others yields to me the secrets of God's amazing plan for me. Healthy fear of this Mighty God, His power to orchestrate my history, is the great inspiration of forgiveness.

I charge you in the presence of God, who gives
life to all things, and of Christ Jesus,
who testified the good confession before Pontius Pilate,
that you keep the commandment without stain or reproach
until the appearing of our Lord Jesus Christ,
which He will bring about at the proper time -
He who is the blessed and only Sovereign,
the King of Kings and Lord of lords,
who alone dwells in unapproachable light,
whom no man has seen or can see.
To Him be honor and eternal dominion!
Amen.
1 Timothy 6:13-16 ESV (emphasis mine)

Created Days

David came to see the wonder of God's unlimited reign.

And he rejoiced at the recognition of
His intimate interest, understanding and
plan for David's existence.

Even before there is a word on my tongue,
Behold, O Lord, You know it all.
You have enclosed me behind and before,
And laid Your hand upon me.
Such knowledge is too wonderful for me;
It is too high, I cannot attain to it.
Psalm 139:4-6 NASB

Our immovable limitations are set in place by our Sovereign Father.

Our many days are under God's sovereign design, and deliberately arranged by Him and not by us.

David came to see the marvel of "God's hand upon Him" and he experienced the bliss of that divine control—
"knowledge too wonderful for me."

Psalm 139:16

HCSB
Your eyes saw me when I was formless;
all my days were written in Your book
and planned before a single one of them began.

AMP

Your eyes have seen my unformed substance;
And in Your book were all written
The days that were appointed for me,
When as yet there was not one of them [even taking shape].

A STORY ALL WRITTEN

Your every day was designed and recorded by God
Himself, before there was any human life.

Imagine!
There is a book written of your life before you live it!

We need only to be glad bondslaves of His will and
the sacred days He created long ago will simply appear.

You can miss it if you like.
But you will lose your significant days and months and
years – of unimaginable adventure and final glory.

God is God and the Only One, but He gives you the
ultimate decision to follow or not. And He will respect
your free choice . . . as also sacred.

Jesus called the Rich Young Ruler to follow,
to go with Him into his own hallowed Story.

But the man turned away from the invitation, as too
costly.

*Looking at him, Jesus felt a love for him and said to him,
"One thing you lack: go and sell all you possess and
give to the poor, and you will have treasure in heaven:
and come, follow Me."*

*But at these words he was saddened,
and he went away grieving,
for he was one who owned much property.
Mark 10:21–22 NASB*

The Rich Young Ruler chose his treasure
        at the expense of his glorious destiny.

This story is told in three of the gospels. Such is its
importance!

(Some like to imagine the man came back.
        It is possible but that is not in the story.
        We must leave it as it is written
        and not create false comfort from a lie.)

Jesus' love for him was undiminished, but His love is the
only existing Love that gives absolute liberty. True to His
Father's gift of freedom, Christ let the man be free to go
his own way, to spend his days *as he wrote them.*

Jesus did not follow him nor plead.

**Such is His Divine Dignity that Jesus stands
ever waiting, but never groveling,
for volunteers to choose their own destiny.**

No Other God

There is neither happenstance nor accident.
There is no other God, nor another Power.
And there is no second cause.

Your Bible is clear about this, and frighteningly so . . .

Joel 2:27b AMP
And that I am the Lord your God,
And there is no other . . .

Isaiah 43:10-11, 13 NASB
"You are My witnesses," declares the Lord,
"And My servant whom I have chosen,
So that you may know and believe Me
And understand that I am He.
Before Me there was no God formed,
And there will be none after Me."

"I, even I, am the L*ORD*,
And there is no savior besides Me."

"Even from eternity I am He,
And there is none who can deliver out of My hand;
I act and who can reverse it?"

NLT
"But you are my witnesses, O Israel!" says the Lord. "You are
my servant. You have been chosen to know me, believe in me,
and understand that I alone am God. There is no other God—
there never has been, and there never will be."

Isaiah 45:5 NASB
I am the Lord, and there is no other; Besides Me there is no God. I will gird you, though you have not known Me.

(See also Deuteronomy 32:39; Isaiah 45:5, 18, 22; 46:9; Joel 2:27)

The Potter and the Wheel

To understand, forgive, and accept *your* sufferings in
life, it is crucial to come to believe in God's absolute
Sovereignty.

The whole universe, the world and all who are in it, exists
for the Son of God Who created it all alongside the Father
in eternities past (Prov. 8:22-31).

God's entire purpose is for His Beloved Son,
in Whom *alone* He is well pleased.

The end toward which God's purpose moves is the
formation of a fitting Bride for Jesus. The marriage of the
Lamb is the culmination of this grand panoramic story of
humanity.

That is the meaning of this universe and of humanity.
You can be part of that purpose or not.
Suffering happens either way.

We don't want this to be true – that God *is* God.
          "I have no power and no control.
                    I don't even know where I am going
                              or why I am suffering!"

Indignation with God is not a problem,
                    He can handle us rebellious ants.

Fight it if you like, you will not prosper.

But who are you, a mere man, to talk back to God?
Will what is formed say to the one who formed it,
"Why did you make me like this?"
Or has the potter no right over the clay, to make from
the same lump one piece of pottery for honor
and another for dishonor?
Romans 9:20-21 HCSB

The great and brilliant sovereignty of God is specific to one purpose: the Lamb. Everything He does has its meaning in the marriage of the Lamb. Life is simply the preparation of the Bride for the Lord Jesus Christ. There is nothing more to this life than that sole and splendid reason.

You have a fascinating part in this greatest of all dramas.

All of your offenses were designed by God for your purification – to be "without spot or wrinkle" – for the position of the Bride. Your injustice is to discourage your hope in humanity. Your pains are meant to cleanse your heart of idols and self.

All disappointments are meant to bring us to the humility of the Lamb nature. And the whole accumulation of our hurts will bring us to a place of transcendent victory, above all the wrongs of this fallen world.

. . . that He might present to Himself the church
in all her glory,
having no spot or wrinkle or any such thing;
but that she would be holy and blameless.
Ephesians 5:27 NASB

Once I suffered a great injustice, a vicious attack railing at me for things I had not done. My heart was broken because it was someone I dearly loved. I couldn't seem to get over it though I prayed and prayed for the grace to forgive. For weeks, I grieved and cried.

Finally, the Lord said to me, "I did it. I sent that person to attack you because for a long time, you felt you needed their love and approval."

A love that needs love cannot purely love.

God's answer both healed me and set me free of the incident. The meaning behind the attack made forgiveness natural. More than even that, the intense pain I felt simply vanished.

At last I could accept the offense because it came from my Beloved!

I had died to this person and therefore I was free of my own needy attachment, set free to love with Christ's intense love. And that happened between us. Christ's love melted me and disarmed my accuser. The power *within* of Christ's loving forgiveness is an irresistible force. Today we enjoy a blessed relationship, founded on the rock of Christ's love.

Joy in the Lord was the fruit and result
of the whole incident!

The assurance of God's sovereignty removes the view that the world is filled with reckless, meaningless cruelty and I am but a helpless victim to it.

All is in order, but it is a divine intention so high and complex that we cannot see it until God reveals Himself.

There is a place beyond forgiveness, the place where God is in total oversight and you can see Him. He reigns above the mess of willful humanity.

Forgiveness is a work of surrender that enables you to see God in His divine purpose – for you!

Joseph came to see the sovereign purpose of his
     unspeakable suffering
     at the hands of his own brothers.

"They meant it for evil."

No doubt as to their motive, but even that Joseph came to accept.

"But God meant it for good."

In the same incident, there were two motives:
one evil and the other good.

The evil was to punish Joseph for his favor from God. Yet that very evil placed Joseph in the arena of his purpose.

The good of God was to save the nation of Israel from starvation.

Joseph's faithfulness to bow through his painful story brought him to the place where God could reveal the unimaginable purpose behind it: to give Joseph the ruling power to save his own people. The meaning of

Joseph's suffering gave him the grace of acceptance and peace, as well as profound wisdom to bring his brothers to repentance and reconciliation with God.

We have also received an inheritance in Him,
predestined according to the purpose
of the One who works out everything
in agreement with the decision of His will.
Ephesians 1:11 HSCB

In the strange power of God – Who rules all events and people for His reigning will – Joseph's brothers were instruments for God's long and deep commitment to Israel. This whole family was woven into an intricate plan for their own salvation. And in the process, they all came to a greater wonder of the knowledge of God as truly, genuinely . . . God.

God is the Potter. I am just the Clay.
The Wheel is the crucible of my mysterious fulfillment.

The Potter can have me.

I will not resist His spinning, molding, and shaping
for the glory of the Lamb.

Living Epistles

You are living within a Love Story,
the Author of Whom is
    making you . . . all about Him!

Joseph and Destiny

Before ever his brothers came to Egypt, Joseph had
forgiven . . . forgiven so deeply that he had entered
God's Sovereign Plan. He was ruling Egypt's wealth with
all the privileges earned by his extraordinary surrender.

Before the years of famine came, two sons were born
to Joseph in Egypt (Gen. 41:50). Joseph gave his sons
significant names that unveiled the secret story of his
traumatic journey to forgiveness.

Joseph named his first son Manasseh and said, "It is
because God has made me forget all my trouble and all
my father's household" (Gen. 41:51).

**Joseph had made his peace with God through
abject surrender in the struggle of
a relationship with the Divine.**

He was at last willing to let go of the family from which
God had removed him. Joseph was building a new family
in his alien home.

The whole story is told by those names.
Profound acceptance lies behind them . . .
and surrender in the extreme.

God has made me forget . . .
Genesis 41:51

The vow to forgive puts the offense in God's hand. Then – only then – He extracts the terrible pain from your soul. When the pain of wrongs is "forgotten" from a memory, the memory itself is irrelevant.

> *. . . those who suffer according to the will of God*
> *shall entrust their souls to a faithful Creator*
> *in doing what is right.*
> *1 Peter 4:19 NASB*

God heals the soul of the one who forgives...

To remember the incident is still possible, but when the pain is gone, what matters the wrong?

Joseph was not trapped by anguish of the past in a cage of bitterness, so the bars in his unjust prison finally opened. He was released into his astonishing "now" and became fully involved in
> *the joy of his presence to God's purpose.*

Forgetting the pain . . . that is the miracle of complete forgiveness, the fruit of God's grace, deeply imbibed by Joseph and permeating to the marrow of his soul.

Mark the cause of Joseph's forgetting. Not his own character, not teeth grinding effort, not mental self-trickery.

> *"God has made me forget . . ."*

> It might be a great human stretch to forgive
> such heinous treatment, but to forget?
> To be free of the terrible suffering?

That is God alone. He bears the hurt so the memory is never intruding itself into today's adventure to ruin it.

**God, the Father of Unending Graciousness,
who longs to forgive and who commits to forget!**

You don't *try* to forget. In forgiving truly, by intimate dealings with God, you simply *will* forget.

This Amazing God extracted from Joseph the excruciating sorrow and anger. As Joseph bowed and clutched Him in desperate pain,
God infused him with His own Divine Forgetting.

". . . all my trouble . . ."

Such trouble as Joseph had makes most suffering pale by comparison. Joseph as our standard, our example of forgiveness, shames us all.

*"God has made me forget all my trouble
and all my father's household."
Genesis 41:51 NASB*

Joseph, thrown out of his family . . . by his family! Great cause of anguish to a Hebrew boy. For the Hebrew man, family was the bedrock of life, the circle of identity. The only sphere of God's blessing.

Joseph was taken from his family and . . .
Joseph let his family go.

What God took, Joseph gave. That! *That*, beloved, is trust that births forgiveness!

> *. . . all my trouble and
> all my father's household . . .*

All. Tiny word speaking volumes, an inclusive and total acceptance by God's grace through His intimate presence, given to a Joseph who sought Him as the only Solution.

> To hurts and wrongs, God is the only hope
> of personal survival and final triumph.
> And forgetting is the proof of
> authentic forgiving.

Joseph named his second son Ephraim and said, *"God has made me fruitful in the land of my suffering"* (Gen. 41:52).

Offenses are the seed and hope of my Destined Fruit. They hold the power of my spiritual prosperity and the secret of God's unimaginable plan for His own vindication to me!

Vindication to prove His Love and Faithfulness to me . . . by the unfolding of His purpose hidden in the offenses. A purpose for my blessing, ONLY.

> **Assault, neglect, betrayal, rejection, violence—
> all God's crucible of preparation . . . to bless.**

Offenses plow the dirt of my soul in furrows I would never choose. God plants the seed of His Idea in that raw earth of my raked soul, but the release of its life and the fullness of its fruit depends entirely on my forgiving and the nurture of my spirit *before* Him, *in* Him, *with* Him.

All this victory,
>   all this forgiveness,
>   came before the famine.

When the famine of Pharaoh's dream and of Joseph's
interpretation arrived, it spread even to Canaan and
captured the tribe of Jacob-Israel.

Starvation covered that entire world and Joseph was the
sole source of survival. The "only one" ready by virtue of
his ability to know God's mind by
>   the long practice of urgent listening.

Joseph ruled as a whole and healed man,
>   made rich by his surrender and
>   reigning over his enemies by the blessing of
>   Sovereign Intervention.

Few of us ever make it out of the prison of Potiphar's
wife: the disgrace and slander of her revenge against
righteousness. It's one thing to be imprisoned guilty, quite
another, innocent.

**Rarely does one so forgive that he is free
of the pain of resistance.**

And oh, so seldom does one become fruitful in the very
place of his oppression and even master of his oppressors.

Such is the reward of the work of forgiveness and the
prosperity in life it yields . . . And! the promise of future
reign with Christ (Rom. 5:17).

RECONCILIATION IS NOT ASSUMED

How stunned Joseph must have been to see his brothers before him, begging for bread in famine.

Here they knelt before him, bowing to his position and to his power over them. And the dream of his youth, long dead, came back . . .

> *Joseph had a dream, and when he told it to his brothers,*
> *they hated him all the more.*
>
> *He said to them, "Please listen to this dream which I have had;*
> *For behold, we were binding sheaves in the field, and lo,*
> *my sheaf rose up and also stood erect; and behold,*
> *your sheaves gathered around*
> *and bowed down to my sheaf."*
>
> *Then his brothers said to him,*
> *"Are you actually going to reign over us?*
> *Or are you really going to rule over us?"*
> *So they hated him even more for his dream*
> *and for his words.*
> *Genesis 37:5-8 NASB*

Now the dream was fulfilled and its symbols clear. The poor sheaves of his brothers' grain were bowing before the provision of Joseph's richer sheaves.

The brothers of treachery had been bound by God!
Forced to bow.

Joseph, bound as well by God, was forced to rise from the cutting of a divine scythe to stand upright, in ruling power over his brothers, true to the dream.

But the brothers were blind to their participation in the dream they scorned, and the presence before them of the dreamer they despised.

This blood brother they had cruelly exiled, was being vindicated as a seer of God and they had no clue.

Their only awareness? Acute hunger.

They did not recognize Joseph in his ruling position. They had sold him as a slave. Such they assumed he still was . . . if alive at all.

And notice please, they did not inquire of this Egyptian Ruler the whereabouts of their lost brother, nor did it seem they made any effort to find him.

They remained indifferent to their brother's plight, still self-saving and self-serving.

Joseph must have waited, even *longed* to hear their concern for him and quest for his restoration, but none came. Yet Joseph stood above them, so broken and tender in spirit that he had to leave their presence and weep.

If he had so forgiven, then why didn't he immediately shout at his brothers, "It's me! Joseph! I'm so glad to see you!"? For this reason:

Forgiveness is not the same as reconciliation.

Joseph wanted his brothers' restoration and that requires repentance, a sorrow of which there was no evidence in them.

I can forgive the person fully for all the wrongs, but reconciliation is the restoring of an alliance, and that requires both persons to be of the same mind and values.

> There is always one Way, one Truth, one Lord.
> Only on that basis can there be true relatedness.

Reconciliation requires that the offender comprehend his offense, know the pain he caused . . . God! And both must come to agreement about the Way, the Truth, and the Life (John 14:6).

> Relationship to anyone is not a "right" we have
> simply because we are Christians.

Friendship is alive only under the Bright Light of God's Truth, of mutual accountability, only in and for Christ's pleasure, and then – of necessity – the cleansing Blood of the Lamb (1 John 1:7).

> **The Christian world believes forgiveness and
> reconciliation are the same thing,
> but restoration does not occur on the heels of
> forgiveness alone.**

Relationships stand only on mutual values and utter honesty, dwelling together under the dominion and love of our reigning Savior-Joseph.

The 'sheaves of our effort' must also be cut down and bound, to bow before Him Who rules.

Reconciliation has to be built with full recognition and accountability for the wrong. On any other ground, true fellowship is dead and forgiveness alone will not resurrect it.

The brothers may have regretted their treatment of Joseph. They may have been in pain over their father's long-term grief. But they had no idea what it was to experience danger and injustice, to be terrified under the power of a cruel foreigner.

Remorseful perhaps, but repentant, no . . .

They could not know the suffering of Joseph by the loss of his homeland. Their actions put Joseph in the place of being imprisoned by a lying accusation and in moral innocence left there for years.

Such an experience was outside even their imagination and certainly not in their sphere of caring. The eleven brothers had always lived by the security of their tribe, under the wealth and God-blessed power of their father.

Never had they experienced the vulnerability and utter aloneness they had forced on Joseph.

Repentance is ever merely partial until we actually enter by empathy the living experience of those we hurt.

God will see to this!

The empathy of "feeling for the affliction of those I hurt" can happen on your knees by the mercy of the Holy Spirit and bring your repentance to full completion.

There being no "experience" because of no kneeling, you might instead find a silver cup in your saddlebag (Gen. 44:1-12).

It was not vengeance on Joseph's part. Revenge would have refused food to them and said, "Starve! You deserve it."

Joseph didn't see his position as a power – at last! – over his brothers or his own long awaited vengeance. He saw his power as a responsibility given by God to help them make it right, for their own sakes. For God's sake.

God trusted Joseph with a position of control over the very existence of his earthly family in order to clear their consciences and restore them to God.

Joseph did not throw his position and victory in his brothers' faces with a vengeful "I have life-and-death power over you."

He did not tout his power but wanted for them all the holy way of moral rectitude. He wanted to bring them not just to peace with himself but with also with themselves, and most of all – above all – with God.

This is a true peacemaker: one who
brings you to peace with God.

Spiritual forgiveness wants more for God
than for oneself.

Joseph had no need for them to see. He had already
solved and resolved his destiny. THEY needed to
understand the living experience of their cruelty.

Joseph forfeited his own agenda, gave up his personal
vendetta, and by amazing self-restraint, he orchestrated
an arena for their understanding in God-given
brilliance . . . all the while never, ever putting them in any
real danger.

Tenderly hiding in the shadows, giving unseen care.
Feeding imprisoned Benjamin from his own table of
proper Jewish food.

> Joseph cared for the souls of his brothers.
> Rarely has the world seen such love,
> such forgiveness.

Joseph loved his brothers enough to forgive them.
Amazing in itself. Humanly rare.
> But that he loved them enough to *restore* them . . .
> *That* is the love and mercy of God Himself.

Reconciliation exists in God's love in Christ, willing to
chasten us in the safety of His shelter that we might
know the effects of our hatred . . . of Him! A hatred
played out on the lovely Josephs of our world.

Daniel and Worship

Surrender is the foundation of forgiveness. And surrender is . . . worship.

Unless the life is bowed to God in utter abandon, forgiving will be a nightmare and a near impossibility.

The life of Daniel is a wonder and a phenomenon. Captured as a teenager, taken to a heathen land and forced to serve, his quiet submission is shocking.

Man of dreams and visions, even visions of God enthroned. Open and living scene of the Son! Rare glimpses into the heavens. Gifted with an "extraordinary spirit" (Daniel 6:3). Exalted to honor by a succession of kings, enemies of each other but friend to Daniel.

To Daniel were entrusted the secrets of history down to the end of the age. He is utterly unique in the annals of the heroes of God.

The secret of Daniel's life was not prayer, though he prayed. Forgiveness was not his centrality and is a word mentioned but twice in his story. And then it was to plead with God to forgive the sins of His people. Faith in God was constantly evident by his gracious and respectful service of his enemy. Forgiveness was a *result* of his faith and worship and not the goal.

Worship was Daniel's life core, the axis of his being.

Under threat of death if he would not worship the king he
served fully with his life's energy,

> *. . . he continued kneeling on his knees three times a day,*
> *praying and giving thanks before his God,*
> *as he had been doing previously.*
> *Daniel 6:10 NASB*

Kneeling, bowing, and looking to God: this is worship.
Daniel prayed and Daniel gave thanksgiving,
but first he knelt in surrender . . .
Surrender *is* worship.

Prayer is a result, not a beginning.
Prayer is secondary.
Worship is the first issue.

Prayer is heard without worship,
but prayer is answered in the realm of worship.

Angels rushed to fight heavenly wars for Daniel's
requests, and they were the highest angels, those who
stood in the very councils of God. Michael, one of the
archangels, was sent to intervene. An angel addressed
Daniel as "greatly loved of God" (Dan. 10:11 NLT). (It
means literally 'desirability or preciousness.') Worship
makes you "desirable and precious" to God!

Daniel's worship, his lifestyle of worship, engaged God's
heart with a special favor that made his prayers instantly
caught up in the heavens.

> *For from the first day . . .*
> *your prayers were heard.*
> *Daniel 10:12 HCSB*

Daniel's secret, the source of all his brilliance and the
power of his character, was his daily, constant worship.

Resistance is solved "on your knees"
by the bowed heart of surrender and devotion to God.

Wisdom is *given* to the worshiper.
Obedience *rises* from worship.
Forgiveness *flows* through worship.

**God's deepest secrets are whispered to
the one who "lives kneeling."**

Daniel's amazing reverence for the cruel kings of his
imprisonment, his constant service without compromise
of his faith—these are humanly impossible!

God's own sterling character, His power of endurance,
flows with richness into the spirit of the one who
worships, who kneels at a daily altar.

We know the story of the lion's den, but we have
overlooked that the issue at stake was worship.
Daniel valued worship more than his own life . . .

Knowing the consequences of the king's edict of death to
all who "petitioned any god or man" other than himself
(Dan. 6:7), Daniel didn't waiver from that which was his
habit, his life focus. With deliberate abandon, he threw
open the windows of his roof chamber to kneel and pray,
knowing his enemies waited and watched for just such a
defiance.

King Darius had been duped into the decree by Daniel's enemies, but such was his esteem and understanding of Daniel, that he pronounced this prophecy:

> *Your God whom you constantly serve*
> *will Himself deliver you.*
> Daniel 6:16 NASB

The king had a peculiar grief over Daniel, since he was the one who was supposedly offended. After the cave was sealed shut with Daniel and the lions inside, the king sealed it with "his own signet ring and the signet rings of his nobles" (v. 17).

In an unheard of compassion among tyrants:

> *Then the king went off to his palace and spent the night fasting,*
> *and no entertainment was brought before him;*
> *and his sleep fled from him.*
> *Then the king arose at dawn, at the break of day,*
> *and went in haste to the lions' den.*
> Daniel 6:18-19 NASB

No bitterness alienated Daniel from his authority. No ill will – always smelled by kings – made Daniel an offense to Darius.

And no rebellion toward his plight offended the Father and prevented the Holy Spirit from executing His highest will, which is always to preserve His children from the danger of the world.

And even more . . .
>to vindicate them in the eyes of their enemies.

The one who gives away his life on the knees of private worship has an immunity and protection, miraculous in nature, full of angelic shields – and that one is safe from the devouring lions of the Enemy.

Forgiveness, flowing out of a life devoted to worship! This is powerful immunity from the evil of your adversary, whether man, lion, or Satan.

Worship of the Highest One is the only safety.

Daniel's focus was on God. Simple and single. He was not obsessed with his poor situation nor his selfish wants. He was not occupied with the evil of the kings he served. He was not embroiled with fighting his deadly enemies.

He set his soul's compass three times a day on
the "Most High God" who ruled
on high over all of it.

The power to endure, insight into the unknown, the wisdom of eternity—all were infused into Daniel through that constant stream of adoring worship . . . rising three times a day to God.

Daniel's Most High God was initiating and responding, flowing back to Daniel's being with His Very Self.

Kneeling to God! A practice Daniel would not abandon for fear of any mere political power of earthly insignificance. And certainly not for fear of his own suffering or death.

Such was Daniel's commitment to worship through his exquisite experience of it. He was placed in the strange position of choosing between his life and his worship.

Daniel could easily choose and readily die,
for he could not live without worship.

**Worship is the source of the power to forgive,
a power which must be Divine . . .
for it is not humanly possible.**

The End of David's Story

DAVID THE KING

David was exalted above all his own story and
remembered at Pentecost as the example of
God's eternal pleasure.

At the Pentecost speech, Peter quotes David speaking of
Christ as before him. No mention of his great sins.

For David says of Him,
'I SAW THE LORD ALWAYS IN MY PRESENCE;
FOR HE IS AT MY RIGHT HAND, SO THAT I WILL NOT BE SHAKEN.
'THEREFORE MY HEART WAS GLAD AND MY TONGUE EXULTED;
MOREOVER MY FLESH ALSO WILL LIVE IN HOPE;

'YOU HAVE MADE KNOWN TO ME THE WAYS OF LIFE;
YOU WILL MAKE ME FULL OF GLADNESS WITH YOUR PRESENCE.'
Acts 2:25-26, 28 NASB

Paul, preaching in Galatia, referred to David by God's
Word:

After He had removed him (Saul),
He raised up David to be their king,
concerning whom He also testified and said,
'I HAVE FOUND DAVID THE SON OF JESSE,
A MAN AFTER MY HEART, WHO WILL DO ALL MY WILL.'
ACTS 13:22 NASB

"But what about . . . ?" No remembrance.

The end of the story *is the story.*

David was formed by the Potter at the hand of Saul, the man's jealous murderer. David survived that mad enemy and learned how not to be king. It takes a Saul to make a David. Thirteen years of assault and attempted murder, a trial so great that most would perish and leave God because of it.

> Then David had his great failures.
> Two sins, shocking and flagrant.

Read Psalm 51, his deep prayers for forgiveness!
A treasure given for all of us sinners.

I won't name David's sins because God doesn't.

When you accept your trials by surrender to God, ever seeking Him, and forgive your enemies, even forgive God for such a fire, you will live in the Kingdom of God's favor. The record of your failures is expunged from the book of your life.

No matter what he did, no matter his mistakes,
David simply kept seeking God. Always.
The Lord was his one desire and his one forever-choice.

> *One thing I have asked from the Lord, that I shall seek:*
> *That I may dwell in the house of the Lord*
> *all the days of my life,*
> *To behold the beauty of the Lord*
> *And to meditate in His temple.*
> *Psalm 27:4 NASB*

David came out in the end of his life with a record of purity and God's eternal pleasure and reward.

The man God created David to be, he finally became – by grace, forgiveness and the sovereign purpose *of Love*. That can be anyone's story.

God obviously did not remember the man's grievous sins of _____. Just as He promised!

Only we readers of the story remember.
But we don't count.

David is proof that it doesn't matter where you start,
or how you stumble.
Where are you going and where do you end?
> That is the final definition of you,
> and the only account of your life.

PRODIGAL PARTY

We are all prodigals.
We lost our destiny and our belonging!
When we come to our senses, do we head home?

Come home to Father with our head bowed
> in the terrible humiliation
> that has produced in us at last, utter humility.

WE have nothing to bring back but our open repentance before heaven and God. And that is all He wants since regret is the only goods we have earned.

Such is the Father's joy that He makes a celebration in the prodigal's honor. Honor?

A ring of authority,
> robe of dignity,
>> sandals of cleanliness,
>>> and a rich celebration for everybody.

A shocking picture of God's loving mercy and grace!
We do not know Him.

How to earn that honor? Come.
The only thing the Lord asks of us in all our dilemmas
and nightmares is simply . . . come to Him.

It means you can fail many times – as we will – and still
have a perfect record and a welcome home. You only need
to come to the Father. He will never coerce you,
but He is ever watching for you to come.

Absolute trust and blessing is bestowed in
> the one who simply . . . **comes to the Father.**

Full restoration and more is the unexpected welcome.

Our story is continuously re-written according to our
repentance. Measured by our forgiving and being
forgiven.

Absolute obedience to God's specific will is the path we
choose and the reward to which we finally arrive. And
Christ will Himself be the obedience required of you.

In the end, your Father will author His own graceful
account of your life, full of His tender mercies
> and Jesus' glory.

You Are a Love Story

You are not some 'poor thing,'
redeemed merely because you have such desperate need.

*For God so **[greatly] loved and dearly prized** the world*
John 3:16 AMP

But God, being [so very] rich in mercy,
because of His great and wonderful love
with which He loved us
Ephesians 2:4 AMP (emphasis mine)

You are saved because of the strange, mystifying,
incomprehensible, unfamiliar, dazzling love of God.

He dreamed you billions of years ago!
And Love bought you at great price
two thousand years ago.

LIVING INSIDE LOVE

Forgiving is not just some legal system for the sake of
control. This is an *Eternal Romance.* YOU are chosen to be
the Lover of One God: Father, Son, and Holy Spirit.

Hate was your inheritance. But Love wants you and
Love will win the battle for you because
Love won you long ago on Calvary.

You were created for Love, to know Love,
to *live inside* that baffling Love God has for such as we . . .

You want to be clean and forgiven –
    to be detached from YOU and the world!
You want the heavens to open
    and the Holy Spirit to have possession of you.
Then you can be a living epistle of the
manifestation of God's Love in Christ, to this world.

By the suffering of your Bloody Savior, you are NOW in
a state of utter holiness, infused with His righteousness.

        Not yet are you living in the splendor of that state,
                though it is all 'in you, IN Him.'

Sin is, above all, separation from God. We are lost and
blind and desperate when we are separated from God by
our own trespasses. We are in a breach with humanity
when we are in a breach with God and more, lost to our
self.

Our Great God has solved that breach – for you, without
you. He is reconciled to you because of Christ. So when
you deal with your sin and your bitterness and shed it
all by the Cross, then you are reconciled with Him. Then
you can *actually* live in that real state of being that Christ
bought when He died for YOU and gave you the gift of
Himself.

Not only are the heavens open for you,
        but you are open to the heavens as Daniel was.

Then you are privy to the fascinating mind of Christ
and filled with the dynamic power of God.
        And you will be caught up into Christ Himself.
                You *experience* being in union with Him.

You watch Him live your life . . . instead of you.

And you will be part of the glorious purpose of Jesus
Christ no matter who you are or who you are not!

We are not the center of all time,
though we silly geese think we are.
    You are not the focus,
        even if you are obsessed with you.
           You are merely the house of Another
               and He can be who He is in you
               once you are an empty vessel.

MORE CHILDREN FOR GOD

> *So now Jesus and the ones he makes holy*
> *have the same Father.*
> *That is why Jesus is not ashamed*
> *to call them his brothers and sisters.*
> Hebrews 2:11 NLT

Jesus is now not ashamed to call you His kin.
    Why? Because He has 'made you holy' and
    you live in His likeness.

YOUR DESIGNER

Would you not love and hover over what you created
with your own hands?

Humanity is like a great Mercedes that a brilliant
    designer meticulously crafted for his delight.

And when it was finished,
    the designer joyfully cranked it up,
    but the car immediately turned on its creator
        and ran him down,
        just to crush him for getting in its way.

In so doing, the beautiful Mercedes totaled itself.

STORY OF ONE

You are living within a Love Story, the Author of whom is
    making you . . . all about Him!

Jesus is the Subject in the stories of all humanity.

THE RICHES OF CHRIST

You have what you do not experience. You live below
your riches. The only obstacle to that is forgiving and
being forgiven.

Don't be so weak and petty, so lily-livered that you won't
tolerate some suffering, meant to prepare you for glory!

Forgive and get on with it.

The Bible says this is the glory that is supposed to be yours,

> *"Christ in you, the hope of glory."*

You are saved not for your sake.
You are redeemed because God loved you so passionately that He sacrificed His greatest Love, Jesus, so you could know the love of God and live rooted deeply in the love of Christ.

What happens in love?
Bliss, exuberant joy, and dreams of the Beloved.

But God, being rich in mercy,
because of His great love with which He loved us,
even when we were dead in our transgressions,
made us alive together with Christ
(by grace you have been saved),
and raised us up with Him, and seated us with Him
in the heavenly places in Christ Jesus,
so that in the ages to come
He might show the surpassing riches of
His grace in kindness toward us in Christ Jesus.
Ephesians 2:4-7 NASB

Afterword

By John Enslow

LIVING WITH GOD IN AN OFFENSIVE WORLD

Life is offensive and filled with offenses. The closer we get to the end of the age, the more offensive it will become. We no longer live in a simple world where we have limited access to humanity's activities. Everything is known and NOW. The world and the offensive things in it come through all of our many electronic devices. If it isn't the television, internet, or radio, it's my phone and watch. It has become impossible to avoid the growing evils of this world.

WEIGHTY OFFENSES

One day I realized that I was becoming weighed down with the barrage of offenses. They were coming in so rapidly that instead of exercising my muscle of forgiveness, I was simply dismissing the offenses. There is a big difference between, "Gah, they're so stupid and evil!" and "Lord, I forgive them for their evil and stupidity!"

In dismissing rather than forgiving offenses, I was missing my interaction and relationship with God through them. It was like living bare skinned on a mosquito farm rather than dwelling in peace? with my God. I was not engaging my heart and spirit in the issues; I was avoiding them and attempting to shoo them away. Ultimately, all this course of action produced was my stewing and festering. I was living inflamed. I had inflammation of the soul which made me touchy and more volatile.

I asked God what to do with this predicament. How do I live in an offensive world, when I have ready access to so many offenses *daily*?

His response to me was, *"Keep a forgiveness journal."*

ACTUAL OFFENSES

In facing my offenses instead of avoiding them, I am becoming freer rather than more entangled. My heart is unburdened. Then it becomes more about my relationship with God and not simply dealing with offenses.

The offenses range from personal interactions to just things that bother me. It really doesn't matter what it is; the criteria is *offenses*. On one hand, it might be a political figure, talking head, or entertainer. On the other, it can be someone much closer in, like a boss, parent, sibling or spouse. Again, it's about my heart, so it's about anything that offends me.

Here's the trick. I'm not to come as an offense inspector; I come to listen. God and I go into situations together and I listen to His mind about what has offended me and how He sees it. What God sees as the true offense might be quite contrary to what has offended me. For example, I might be offended by someone's abuse of me, and God might say that their true offense is bitterness with Him. By inquiring of the Lord as to what the offense actually is, I involve Jesus and begin to see it as He does. It might start as mine but as I pray through the offense, it becomes His to resolve.

It isn't that God dismisses my offenses as unimportant or trivial. He doesn't. But if I'm forgiving someone for mistreating me, and God says they're scorning the Life of Christ . . . then my mistreatment kind of falls by the wayside in light of their true offense. They are in so much more trouble than merely offending me.

In short, God's view of offenses very often overshadows my personal "ouchies." Not always, but sometimes it isn't about forgiving slights against me. My forgiveness journal is about taking all my heart to my Father. It is about our relationship and His involvement in my life.

LIFTING THE WEIGHT

In practice, I start by writing down my personal wounds and then listening for how God feels about them. This way my hurt doesn't lie festering in me like a thorn. It's easier when I get it written down and out of my heart and head. When I can look at it in print, I might even find that I am offended with something quite different than I first thought. Writing it out is therapeutic to see what's in the deep corners of my heart and mind. And as I am getting it down, I am listening: What will God say? How will the Spirit move on this situation? Is my offense even real or have I made something out of nothing? The whole process is an invitation for God to come into my heart and life, and it then becomes a very tangible first step toward forgiving.

This is how the Father has led me. I do this on my iPhone in a journaling program, and I include a picture of the offender. My phone is always with me and that's just one less thing I have to carry, but any method of journaling would work. The journal of forgiveness has been good for me and for my heart. I am emotionally lighter and less volatile. The process is keeping me current and honest and involved with God's mind, not just mine.

My motivation is relationship with God and staying current in my heart. I don't want anything to separate me from my God, and offenses are walls and barriers to my relationship with Him.

THE FRUIT OF THE JOURNAL

The fruit of my journal has been vast, from greater intimacy with God to emotional freedom. I've had negative and volatile situations literally work themselves out. After taking it to God, He brought resolution and healing to offensive situations even without my direct interaction. This doesn't mean I can always avoid conflict, but His Way paved through all the landmines is better than my bull-in-a-china-closet. And it has gone from the most minuscule hating of someone's face on TV to being completely unaffected or involved. In a word, *freedom.*

In our world of evil, the love of most is growing cold. I believe in part that this is because we're becoming crushed with offenses that we shrug off rather than forgive. It's just a breeding ground for the demonic torment of unforgiveness.

Keeping close to God and current in my heart with all that offends me has opened the way to loving Him. Remaining current through a forgiveness journal is like living under a blue-skied, crisp fall day rather than sweating beneath a hot muggy summer afternoon.

And beyond how it affects my soul, I become a fount of Christ's forgiveness into a world of unforgiveness.

Offenses are an *invitation* to be involved with God, not something to be avoided. God is saying, "Face the situation and bring ME into it." **I am an ambassador for Christ, so every situation is an opportunity for me to bring Christ in.** I am here for HIM and He wants entrance into my world through me. While He is the Way, I am a door for Him to enter in to this world.

Who is a God like you, who pardons sin and forgives the transgression of the remnant of His inheritance? You do not stay angry forever but delight to show mercy. You will again have compassion on us; You will tread our sins underfoot and hurl all our iniquities into the depths of the sea.
Micah 7:18-19 NIV

Author's Notes

Throughout this book, I refer to Strong's and Louw-Nida for a deeper understanding of the scriptures I cite. Here is the bibliography for these two sources.

Johannes P. Louw and Eugene A. Nida. *Greek-English Lexicon of the New Testament Based on Semantic Domains.* New York: United Bible Societies, 1988.

James Strong. *The Exhaustive Concordance of the Bible (Strong's Concordance).* 1890.

Surprisingly real, refreshingly unfiltered

The Shulamite Podcast

Check out our weekly podcast!

The joys and sufferings, triumphs and stumblings of living life as a child of God...

Come sit down with Martha, John and the rest of the Shulamites as we delight in our amazing God and discuss the practical side of discipleship from our daily lives and relationships with Jesus Christ.

Available online at
www.shulamitepodcast.com
or through iTunes